Ripping The Roof Off Real Estate

It's Not What You Save
It's What You Keep

Mollie W. Wasserman

Gabriel Publications
14340 Addison Street Suite 101
Sherman Oaks, CA 91423
Visit our website at www.GabrielBooks.com
Or call 800-940-2622

Ripping the roof off real estate: it's not what you save, it's
what you keep / Mollie W. Wasserman

ISBN-13: 978-1-60026-012-4
ISBN-10: 1-60026-012-8
Library of Congress Catalog Card Number 2006934948

Book designed by www.KarenRoss.com
Edited by Kate Shaffar
Publisher Simon Rawlinson

Printed in the United States of America

This book is dedicated to:
Nice folks who would like to get quality
and value for their real estate dollar, while
realizing the most profit when they sell their home.
AND
All hardworking real estate agents who strive every day
to take the best care of their clients and who
want to be paid fairly for their services, time, and the
expertise that can only come from years of experience.

Warning

This book will challenge many widely held myths about real estate. You will be exposed to the straight facts (and a lot of strong opinions), but absolutely no sales spiel. Those of us "in the trenches," have seen, over the years, where real estate value is won and where it is lost, where the public, responding to the hype put out by hucksters in misleading ads and sensational "news" articles, pick up pennies only to drop dollars. It's time that the consumer is honestly informed about the real workings of real estate, where and how to spend their hard-earned money, and where not to waste their energy and time.

It is also time for consumers, as well as the real estate industry, to begin regarding and compensating agents as the true professional consultants they are, rather than as salespeople simply selling a product to generate a sales commission.

When all is said and done, my passion and goal in writing this book, is to get the word out that in real estate—as is true in other fiduciary fields such as finance and law—*experience, knowledge, and expertise are not expensive—they are priceless.*

Hopefully when you finish this book, I will have made the case that when it comes to getting your best value in real estate:

It's not what you save, it's what you keep!

Mollie W. Wasserman
Framingham, Massachusetts
October 2006

Table of Contents

Preface
Acknowledgments
Disclaimer
About the Term Realtor®
About the Author
Introduction: An Industry with an Identity Crisis

PART 1: The Current State of Real Estate

PART 2: How About Some Choices?

PART 3: The Four Financial Potholes

Preface

I have a saying taped to my desk, right next to my computer that I look at almost daily:

God, grant me the strength to fight the good fight
Not because it's always winnable, but because it
needs to be fought.

There's not a day that I read this verse when I don't immediately think of my dad and how, as I was growing up, he taught me through his example to "fight the good fight no matter the consequences."

For the past 12 years, as I've experimented with different compensation options and a whole new way of looking at my industry, I've heard my share of negative comments such as, "Real estate has always been paid by commission." Or, "This is the way we've always done it."

I take comfort in the following *absolutes* expressed over the years:

"This telephone has too many shortcomings to be seriously considered as a means of communication. The device is inherently of no value to us."
—internal Western Union memo, 1876

"Everything that can be invented has already been invented."
—Charles H. Duell, director of the U.S. Patent Office, 1899

"Who the hell wants to hear actors talk?"
—H.M. Warner, Warner Brothers, 1927

"I think there is a world market for maybe five computers."
—IBM chairman Thomas Watson, 1943

Change is difficult and takes time. Changing an entire industry from one where real estate salespeople are paid to move product, to one where real estate consultants are paid to provide counsel, guidance, and care to people looking to buy or sell their largest financial asset is, I believe, a fight that needs to be fought.

Is it winnable? Perhaps, but I hold no illusions that the radical ideas that I present in this book are going to be adopted, by either the public or the real estate industry itself, in the near future. Shoot, they might not be adopted in my lifetime.

But as President John F. Kennedy said so eloquently in his inaugural address on January 20, 1961 when speaking of the many goals he wished our country to reach:

> All this will not be finished in the first 100 days. Nor will it be finished in the first 1,000 days, nor in the life of this Administration, nor even perhaps in our lifetime on this planet. But let us begin.

Acknowledgments

It is impossible to thank everyone who, over the years, has contributed to my growth and therefore to making this book possible. Nevertheless, I will try.

To my publisher, **Rennie Gabriel**, who took a big risk on my crazy ideas, and provided the backing that brought life not only to this book, but also an online Consulting Course for Realtors®.

To my editor, **Simon Rawlinson**, who took my words and made them sing.

To my partners in bringing the Consulting Model to hardworking Realtors® everywhere: **Paula Bean** of Carib-Gulf Realty and **Tom Pickering** of the Tek Café.

To my attorney **Brendan Radigan** for reviewing and drafting the publishing agreements that made this book possible. And thanks to both Brendan & his wife **Tricia** for their friendship.

To **Karen Stefani**, who no matter how long we go between visits, picks up the conversation where we left off.

To **Betsy Robinson** of Greenpark Mortgage, for keeping me laughing when times got tough.

To the wonderful members of my real estate team:

Dina Raneri, whose enthusiasm and hard work is a joy to watch.

Yolanda Evangelista, who has overcome more obstacles than many of us will face in a lifetime, is wise beyond her years, and whom I am proud to call my friend.

Lisa Feldman, my business partner and "alter-ego" who is always there for me through thick and thin.

Last, but certainly not least, I am forever grateful to my family.

To my husband **Steve**, who has provided me the encouragement and support to reach for the stars and who, in his own quiet way, has always been my biggest fan.

To my sons **Jeffrey** and **Daniel** who have developed each in their own way into very special young men, for keeping me grounded and constantly reminding me of what's important.

To my parents for teaching me that while a reputation can be won or lost in a day, one's good character is built over a lifetime. To my mom, **Anita Woolf**, for raising me to believe in myself even though my talents are quite different from hers. To my dad, **Ken Woolf**, for showing me through his example, that it's okay to think "out of the box."

To my sisters, **Sherri Noble** and **Lisa Ploss**, who always have my back and are right in my corner.

To my in-laws, **Reuben and Rosalind Wasserman**, who have always shared with me the value in family.

And in loving memory of my grandparents:

To my grandmother **Jo Woolf** who, along with my mom, was always a testament to a woman's strength, long before it was fashionable. And to my grandfather, **Cy Woolf**, who always called me his "rubber ball" in encouraging the resiliency of my character.

"When a man does not keep pace with his companions, perhaps he is marching to the beat of a different drummer."

——**Henry David Thorough**

"People are always blaming their circumstances for what they are. I don't believe in circumstances. The people who get on in this world are those who go out and find their circumstances. And if they can't find them, they make them."

——**George Bernard Shaw**, *Mrs. Warren's Profession*

Disclaimer

We have attempted to ensure that everything said here is accurate and relevant. However, laws change, circumstances vary, home prices and interest rates change, and there is the possibility for error. Using the guidance offered here, along with your selection of a competent real estate professional, you should feel confident in purchasing or selling real estate. This text should be used only as a general guide and not as the ultimate source of real estate information. We are not providing accounting, legal, or tax advice in this book. We recommend that you hire an attorney or other appropriate professional who can assist with the specifics involved in any legal or tax matter. The publisher and author shall have neither liability nor responsibility to any person or entity with respect to any loss or damage caused, directly or indirectly, by the information contained in this book.

About the Term Realtor®

You will notice that I use the term *Realtor*® often in this book, and when I do, the registration mark is used. There is a reason for that. The term Realtor® is a trademark of the National Association of REALTORS® (NAR), and any agent or broker who uses this term as part of their professional identity must be a member, not only of NAR but also of their state and local associations.

NAR members have training that is only available to its members. They have the benefit of local meetings and state and national conferences where they can network with other Realtors®. Many transactions are actually put together for buyers and sellers at these events.

But why should you care? This is why: Realtors® subscribe to a code of ethics, which commits them to conduct their business with a sense of fair play. The public has some recourse when they feel they have been lied to, mistreated, or cheated. They can file an ethics complaint with the local association requesting the Realtor® be disciplined, or request arbitration if they feel they have actually been cheated out of money. The Grievance Committee and the Professional Standards Committee of the organization handle these complaints. While a member is not bound to submit to the grievance process when a complaint is initiated by buyers or sellers, most do because it is a much simpler and less costly method of justice than going to court.

Members pay dues, and other fees to maintain a membership in good standing, but the bottom line is that they are in a position to provide much better service to you than non-members. Agents and brokers that do not have the Realtor® designation are operating independently. They often do not do enough business to justify the costs involved in belonging to NAR, and their professional actions are not governed by its code of ethics.

For starters, when hiring someone to assist you in the purchase or sale of your largest financial asset, get a Realtor®.

My thanks to friend and colleague, Ken Deshaies, for this important explanation of the term Realtor® *and why it is important to the consumer.*

About the Author

Mollie Wasserman is an Accredited Buyer Representative (ABR), an e-PRO 500 (Select 50) Certified Internet Professional, an iSucceed Mentor, as well as one of only 200 CyberStars™ around the world—an elite group of Realtors® who generate a significant portion of their business through the use of current technology. A believer in continuing education, she has taken advanced courses and holds a broker's license. She is also the coauthor of *How to Make Your* Realtor® *Get You the Best Deal: Massachusetts Edition.*

Mollie has always loved to play matchmaker—identifying people's needs and finding just the right products or services to match them. She has utilized her unique marketing talents and outgoing personality in order to successfully represent hundreds of buyers and sellers and assist them in reaching their goals. Her four-person team, The Home Consultants Realty Team, services over 50 cities and towns in Greater Boston's western and southwestern suburbs, and is affiliated with Keller Williams Realty.

Mollie has been at the forefront of real estate technology from the beginning of her real estate career, having designed her first website in late 1995. In March of 1996 MollieW.com (now www.MetroWestRealty.com) went online and has since received much national recognition, including being featured in, *Banker & Tradesman*, Forbes.com, Money.com, and *Realtor® Magazine* (formerly *Today's Realtor®*). In 1998, Mollie was profiled in Intel's research paper on the transformation of the real estate industry which called her "the agent of the future." Her team's site has also been awarded "Top 10" by the *International Real Estate Digest* (IRED).

She is known as a pioneer in the development of "Real Estate Consulting"—a new, innovative business model in real estate that shifts the focus from sales to consulting, and provides compensation alternatives to commissions. In 2002, she added a new site, www.MyREConsultants.com, which is devoted to providing consumers with information regarding real estate consulting and fee-based options. Mollie, along with her partners Tom Pickering and Paula Bean, are the developers of a new, online course due out in the fall of 2006, which guides the real estate professional in developing the consulting model in their own practice. Successful completion of this course leads to the designation, Accredited Consultant in Real Estate™ (ACRE).

Mollie is multi-geographic, having been born in Florida (of Boston-bred parents) and raised in Texas. She attended school in Florida, Pennsylvania, and Mississippi before coming to the Boston area in 1979. She and her husband, Steve live in Framingham, Massachusetts with their two teenage sons, Jeff and Dan, and a very cute Cavalier King Charles Spaniel named, Kirby.

Mollie holds a BA in mass communications from the University of Southern Mississippi and an MBA with a concentration in marketing from Northeastern University. She is a licensed Emergency Medical Technician (EMT) and looks forward to continuing her studies in Paramedicine.

In her free time she enjoys cooking with Jeff, playing guitar with Dan, and rooting for her beloved Red Sox, Celtics, and Patriots.

An Industry with an Identity Crisis

A few years back, my business partner, Lisa Feldman, mused:

> You know, Mollie, I know we've talked about this before, but I'm finding it more and more difficult to get buyers to sign a buyer agency contract. I explain that this agreement will allow me to represent their interest rather than the seller's, but they are still so reluctant.

I nodded my head because this has been my experience over the last few years. It seems that in the age of the Internet, people are getting phobic about their privacy as well as being increasingly nervous about making commitments. No matter how it's explained, contracts just seem to scare people. A buyer agency contract, as Lisa and I explain to potential homebuyers, is simply a contractual relationship that puts in writing that the agent must work in the *buyer's* best interest.

But later on that same day that Lisa and I were speaking, a light bulb went on in my head. What if the real estate industry had been missing the boat this whole time? What if we had been reading the public wrong? Maybe the real estate consumer wasn't at all scared of signing contracts, but rather just befuddled as to whom they were dealing with when they wanted to buy or sell a home? All of a sudden, I glimpsed what might be going through their minds:

> *Who is this real estate agent in front of me? What are they anyway? Are they a salesperson trying to sell me a house, or are they some kind of consultant offering to represent my needs? If they are a salesperson, shouldn't they just be trying to sell me a property? What is all this talk about providing representation? And if they're a consultant I'm paying to represent my needs, then why is the amount of their compensation, or whether they get paid at all, wholly dependent on my decision or how much I spend?*

This got me thinking. When I, as a consumer, deal with salespeople versus consultants, what are my expectations of each?

Suppose I want to buy a car. If I enter a showroom, I would expect someone to walk up and offer to help me. I would immediately identify that "someone" as a salesperson. My expectation would be that they would ask about my needs—the make of the car, model, color, features that I'm interested in. Then they should show me cars that might match those needs. Since I have a high regard for good salespeople, I would have the expectation that they would deal with me honestly and not misrepresent themselves, the dealership, or their vehicles. However, I would harbor no illusions that they were working for anyone other than their dealership and themselves.

But suppose that when I entered the showroom, someone came up and instead of showing me cars, whipped out a contract and said, "Before I start showing you around, I'd like you to consider signing this contract. By doing so, I can represent your interest rather than that of the dealership. And even though I'm paid by commission, signing this contract will allow me to negotiate the best deal on whatever car you decide to buy." If this happened, I would be really confused, and frankly, a bit skeptical.

This person wants to represent my needs and negotiate the best deal for me on a car, yet the amount of their compensation—or whether they get paid at all—is wholly dependent on my decision. And how is it that he will use his skills to negotiate the lowest price when he is paid as a percentage of what I end up paying?

That got me thinking about another scenario. Suppose I was having legal concerns regarding my finances. I would make an appointment to meet with a qualified attorney, and my expectation would be that I would pay that attorney for a consultation either by an hourly fee or a flat rate. I would expect that they would use their expertise to advise me regarding my financial issues and assist me in a resolution. And because I was paying them for their time, expertise, and experience, I would most definitely have the expectation that their counsel would be completely objective.

Yet suppose during the consultation, the attorney started discussing some financial products that she sold on the side. "Instead of paying me by fee, you can buy one of these products. I'll get a commission on whatever I sell you and you'll end up paying less."

If this happened, not only would I be confused, I'd be out of there! My expectation was that I was hiring a professional to consult *with* me, not to sell *to* me. And I would be very skeptical about this attorney giving me truly objective advice if her pay was contingent on selling me something and on how much I spend overall.

Make no mistake, folks: The real estate industry, in this first decade of the 21st century, is having an identity crisis because agents are being asked to fill two roles which are in conflict, especially in the mind of the consumer.

On one hand, real estate has always been considered a sales profession, paid by commission. The fact is that as an independent contractor, a real estate agent needs to move the "inventory" as quickly as possible, and for as much money as possible, if they want to make a living in this business.

And yet, if an agent is a Realtor® (most, but not all agents are, so make sure that the one you deal with *is*), they must follow a code of ethics which, among other things, requires them to put the needs and interests of their clients ahead of everyone else's, including and most especially, their own. Staying poised and performing in these two conflicting roles is an incredible balancing act, but I'm here to tell you that the overwhelming majority of my fellow agents walk that line everyday and they walk it well.

Despite what you might hear in the popular press (more on this later), most real estate agents are hardworking, honest, and ethical professionals who strive—sometimes at great financial sacrifice—to do right by their clients.

When working with a seller, most agents will recommend a listing price that will get the seller the most money in a reasonable period of time, when under pricing it, the home would sell faster and they could be assured of being paid. Hence, the conflict of interest. Most listing agents will truthfully counsel a seller on what the market is doing. They may even suggest a seller not sell their home when the market doesn't favor a profitable sale, even though they only get paid if the seller does. When a seller has outgrown their home, I have known many an agent who has counseled them to remodel rather than move, even though they have just talked themselves out of a job.

Now, let's look at the other side. When working with homebuyers, buyer agents (who have a contractual obligation to work in their buyer's best interest) *do every day what makes absolutely no sense on paper:* Negotiate the lowest possible price for their buyer-clients even though they are paid as a percentage of that price.

The fact that the vast majority of agents routinely put the needs and interests of their clients before their own is a testament to the industry and makes me very proud, but agents are doing so *in spite of* the commission system, not because of it.

One of the most common questions I receive from sellers is: *How do I know that you are pricing my home for the best value rather than the speed of closing the sale?* And one of the most common questions from buyers is: *Why would you negotiate the best deal for me when you get more money from a higher sale price?* I answer both the same: "My business is built on referral. A few extra dollars in my pocket isn't going to mean beans when you find out that you sold for too little (sellers) or paid too much (buyers)." But while my answer is sound and reflects how I work, it still begs the questions of the inherent conflict of interest when you're compensated for moving product while charged with giving objective counsel.

"Please, Just Tell Me What I'm Paying For!"

In the same way that most agents are hardworking folks who strive to do right by their clients, my experience is that the vast majority of consumers appreciate what a good real estate professional brings to the table. They have no problem with paying for quality real estate assistance, *if only they could make sense of what they are paying for.*

If you're like most consumers, you probably have never really understood how the commission system works. Today, with housing prices having risen so fast, a 5, 6, or 7 percent commission can sometimes amount to more than the equity in your home. When the economy is good, home sellers may silently wonder about the commission system, but when the economy tightens, they increasingly become vocal and start asking agents some very logical questions:

- If I price my home where you tell me to, get it in tip-top condition, and make it easy to show, why am I paying the same thing as the guy down the street who does none of these things?
- When my $600,000 home sells, I will be paying twice as much as my cousin across town who is selling a $300,000 home. Why is that? Do you do twice as much work? Or put in twice as much time?

When agents complain to their brokers that it's getting more and more difficult to justify their commissions to the public, brokers overwhelmingly just tell them to show the client how much they do for them. And while I would agree that much of the public has no idea how much work is involved with selling a home, trotting out a list of the *450 Things That an Agent Does* misses the point.

As we'll see in a later chapter, paying by commission has nothing to do with compensating an agent for time or services. *Commissions are all about mitigating risk.* Until we, as an industry, are willing to call it what it is, and provide choices, we agents will continue to see our compensation erode and our value undermined while consumers are increasingly left on their own without necessary services, expertise, or representation when selling what is, for the majority of people, their largest financial asset.

Let's face it, sometimes consumers have real estate needs that don't lend themselves to the *traditional full-marketing-package-payable-only-by-commission* model. For example:

Maybe the consumer happened to find an interested buyer on their own, but they need expert assistance in negotiating, troubleshooting, and managing the transaction until it closes.

Maybe they've outgrown their home (or their house has outgrown them) and they need objective counsel on whether to *move* or *improve*.

Or, maybe they have no desire to play Realtor®, and they need a full package of services, but would like to pay the real estate professional for whatever is rendered, the way they pay for most other service providers.

I believe it's high time that the consumer be offered real choices in what services they want and how they would like to pay for them, as long as they understand three basic economic realities which I'll detail more later:

1. High risk means high reward. If you, as a consumer, want the agent to take all the risk (i.e., you only want to pay an agent if you get your desired outcome), then you're going to have to pay a premium for that safety net.

2. On the other hand, if you would rather pay for an agent's services, expertise, and time rather than a convoluted percentage of your home's sale price, you can't have that compensation be contingent on the sale. Just like any other service provider, if they provide the services and time, they need to be paid for them.

3. If you only want to pay for a six-pack of beer, don't expect to receive a bottle of champagne. You get what you pay for. And in real estate, it's

very easy to be enticed to go cheap, and becomes evident that when you do, overwhelmingly, you will save pennies, but drop dollars.

At the same time, I also believe that it's high time that hardworking agents stop working (and advertising their services) for free. Nothing in this world is free; not a market analysis advertised in the paper nor the "tour guide services" that agents routinely provide buyers with no assurance that the buyer will actually buy a home, and if they do, buy a home with them. Unpaid hours of work need to be made up somewhere, and under the commission system, they are made up by the transactions that actually do close.

The White Elephant in the Room

No matter how it's presented or dressed up, there is an inherent conflict of interest when an agent is expected to act as a fiduciary agent providing objective, unbiased counsel to clients, while at the same time being paid by commission. This unspoken reality, combined with a lack of choices in the real estate services offered and how they can be paid for, is the white elephant in the room. The real estate industry knows it's there because the consumer keeps pointing to it, but no one wants to acknowledge it and certainly no one wants to talk about it. The industry has instead become expert at creating diversions, such as skimming a percentage point off the commission when the consumer complains, or charging an "administrative fee" to try to cover their costs, but these diversions are temporary and beg the very real questions.

The industry nibbles at the corners because resolving the real issues requires a major paradigm shift in how we define ourselves as agents and as an industry. It means a new way of thinking and acting, developing a whole new model in real estate. Dealing with the real issues means looking the consumer in the eye and telling them the truth:

Yes, commissions *are* high—they have to be! It's the price a consumer must pay if they want the agent and their broker to take the risk.

The white elephant is growing, and to continue to ignore its presence is to see a future of decreasing compensation for hardworking agents, while leaving the public priced out of vital services and representation and at the mercy of hucksters who would have them believe that selling a home is no more difficult than selling used clothes at a yard sale.

One of my favorite books is, *Sacred Cows Make the Best Burgers* by Robert Kriegel and David Brand. They explain why when tradition fails, it's time for change. I didn't write this book so bookstores would have another real estate how-to on their shelves. Frankly, there are enough real estate books on the shelves already, and sadly, most of them are either useless or downright misleading, written by people who have no clue as to how real estate really works.

No, I wrote this book because it's time that we talk straight and clear and lay our cards on the table. It's time that the public is given a clear picture of what it's really like to be a real estate agent today. Conversely, it's time for the real estate industry to start *really listening* to what the consumer is saying and what they're asking for.

Agents need to stop selling and start consulting. The public deserves it and so does the hardworking agent.

PART I:

The Current State of Real Estate

CHAPTER I

How in the World did We Get Here?

A Short History

There doesn't seem to be an exact date that real estate, as we know it, began. Clearly, the practices of buying and selling one's property probably dates back to the end of the middle ages when property ownership passed from lords to common people. The job of matching sellers and buyers of property for compensation has more than likely existed in some form since then.

What has become today's National Association of REALTORS® was originally formed in 1908 as the National Association of Real Estate Exchanges with the objective of, "uniting the real estate men of America for the purpose of effectively exerting influence upon matters affecting real estate interests." In other words, these real estate guys formed what sounds like a trade union to advocate for, and protect their own interests. At this juncture, the "public interest" does not appear to be an objective of this group.

It's important to know that prior to 1908 licensing laws didn't exist and the real estate industry had a history of speculation and disorder. The new association did begin to regulate the practice of real estate. In 1913, this group, now known as the National Association of Real Estate Boards, adopted a Code of Ethics, with the Golden Rule as its theme. While it states a goal of protecting the public interest, the primary focus of the Code of Ethics was providing guidelines for arbitrating monetary disputes between Realtors®, as well as providing the basis for licensing laws. At this time real estate could not be defined as anything but a sales profession. While licensing laws began to protect the public from the most blatant exploitation, "buyer beware" was the rule. There was no representation, or fiduciary responsibility, as we know it.

In fact, until World War II, selling a home was no different than selling any other product. There was no agency, and therefore, no fiduciary responsibilities. An agent could show a prospective buyer a home in a truly "tour guide" role, by demonstrating features and benefits. There were little, if any, disclosure requirements, as we know them now.

After World War II, the concept of agency with the attendant protection and promotion of the interests of the client became a more prominent consideration. This was the beginning of the dual role of the agent: first as a salesperson with a goal of selling properties, and second, as that of a fiduciary, protecting the interest of the client.

Still, from the 1940s through the 1980s, the focus was on sales. After all, the only client was the seller and protecting their interests consisted primarily of getting them the most money for their property. There was little, if any, knowledge of environmental risks that must be disclosed, and, of course, the buyer had no representation. In addition, housing prices were much more in line with other necessities of life so a 6 or 7 percent commission was rarely questioned.

In the mid-eighties, the agent's role as a fiduciary began to grow. Knowledge and required disclosure of items such as Urea-Formaldehyde Foam Insulation (UFFI) and lead paint began. While buyer representation was still largely unheard of, more and more states were requiring that agents and their brokers disclose that they were working in the interest of the seller.

Of course, the mid-eighties brought a rapid increase in home prices (which later crashed) putting downward pressure on commissions since they now represented a far larger expense to the seller. The traditional sales model that had been in use for over 75 years was beginning to develop cracks. While there was little issue yet of conflicts of interest, sellers increasingly began questioning what they were paying for and why it was so much when they paid by commission.

As the 1990s dawned, the dual forces of: a.) a rapid growth of buyer representation, and b.) little or no change in the basic sales model and approach brought about conflicts in the consumer's mind.

But the problems ran deeper. The consumer's perception of the agent as a salesperson paid by commission went hand in glove with that of the agent's value being one of a gatekeeper of information. The emphasis on the role of salesperson rather than one of an advisor contributed the public's belief that the agent was simply the *provider* of information rather than an *interpreter*.

The focus of the public was on the agent as a functionary rather than that of a fiduciary (more on this in a later chapter). As the Internet grew and access to information exploded, the Internet-savvy consumer increasingly believed that the real estate agent was replaceable. And today, in the era of eBay, craigslist.com, and almost universal access to the Multiple Listing Service (MLS), if an agent's role is solely that of a salesperson, providing access to the "inventory," then their job is truly endangered.

If that was the whole story, then there wouldn't be a need for this book. But with all the emphasis on the agent as a salesperson gathering information and providing functionary (and therefore replaceable) services, little attention has been paid to the more important role that a real estate professional plays. That role is one of a consultant and an advocate with a value that can never be replaced by technology: taking that mound of data that can be obtained so easily nowadays and interpreting what it all means to the benefit of the client.

Let's fast-forward to today. The public has increasingly missed the boat on where the value of a real estate professional lies, with the result of a prevalent "do-it-yourself" mentality that has overwhelmingly not led to cost savings, but lost time and money.

This is not the public's fault! Certainly the press has not helped with damning articles about real estate agents and their "salesperson" mentality, but the real culprit out there is the real estate industry itself. The business of real estate has changed incredibly over the last hundred years, but the sales model and practice has not. There are many of us who think it's time it did.

CHAPTER 2

The Other Side of the Fence

Growing up, one of the sayings I heard most was: *Don't judge the next tribe until you've walked a mile in their moccasins.* There are a lot of variations of this saying, yet the message is still very clear and important. I think it's human nature to make observations and sometimes to generalize about another group of people; this is often how we make sense of the world. Unfortunately, this practice leads to stereotypes, which have no connection to reality.

In talking with hundreds of consumers over the years, it's clear to me that many have misconceptions about how real estate works, how homes get bought and sold, and how easy (or not) it is for a real estate agent to make a living in this business. Fed by advertising "come-ons" promising the world for a song and inaccurate articles about the industry masquerading as news, many consumers have developed a false impression about real estate. Without valid and complete information, many consumers have embarked upon buying or selling a home with discounters or completely on their own, without advocacy or representation. With the vast majority of them losing—rather than saving—their precious time and money.

At the same time, it's abundantly clear that the real estate industry has done an incredibly poor job of listening to the consumer. Instead of coming up with real options that give the consumer value for their dollar and flexibility in how they pay for real estate services, real estate companies either stubbornly stick to offering only the standard *full-marketing-package-paid-only-by-full-commission*. Or they offer discount commissions with shoddy, discount services that don't get the job done, thereby further eroding the value of the real estate professional in the consumer's mind.

In the interest of developing some understanding between the parties, let's look at the following sections, A Day in the Life Of a Realtor®, and A Decision for Consumers. Obviously, both Realtor® Joe Davis and the consumers, are fictional and their experiences a composite, but I can assure you that every one of their experiences I have either personally lived through, or has been related to me by others.

A Day in the Life of a Realtor®

Joe Davis

Chicago, Illinois

Nine Years in Real Estate

6:00 A.M.

When the alarm goes off, Joe Davis rises quickly. Today promises to be a busy day, which is a rare commodity lately since the market started to tank last year. But today his calendar is full. He has a meeting with some new buyers first thing this morning, followed by a broker open house that he's hosting on one of his listings. Then, in the early afternoon he has a house-hunting trip scheduled with some other buyers that he has been working with for a while (it seems like he's been working with them forever). Later this afternoon, he has a listing appointment. In between, he has a ton of phone calls to make and paperwork to do, for the twelve listings he has as well as the four transactions he has in process.

7:15 A.M.

Before leaving the house, Joe checks his email and finds one from a potential client about selling his house. Joe's hopes begin to rise until he sees the "To" line which says, "Undisclosed Recipient." That can only mean one thing—this seller has sent out this standard email to many other agents. As Joe begins to read it, he realizes why. This seller just wants to know what commission Joe charges and "how low will Joe go." It's clear that this seller is just shopping agents by price and Joe is not going down *that* road again. He knows he can't win on price—no matter how low he goes, in this market, some agent will always go lower. He actually saw an ad last week from an agent offering to list homes for *free*. Joe shakes his head and says aloud, "I may be desperate, but I'm not crazy!" He deletes the email.

7:23 A.M.

He checks his voicemail and finds a message from another seller wanting to know if Joe could come over and meet with him tomorrow night. Joe thinks it would be difficult to get a market analysis done that quickly, but he *could* do it. Then he remembers that his daughter's toddler recital is tomorrow night. He calls the seller back and explains that he'd love to come over but unfortunately has a family commitment tomorrow night. Can he schedule for another time? "Sorry," says the seller. "If you want a chance at my listing, it's tomorrow night or nothing." Joe says he's sorry, but his family is his priority. He sits there and wonders if there is any field other than real estate, where you're expected to be available 24/7 with no personal life.

7:45 A.M.

He drives to his office for his buyer meeting thinking that the buyers he's meeting with, sounded tough on the phone yesterday. They called him because they saw a house for sale in the paper and wanted him to show it to them. He explained that it would be far more time efficient if they met with him first. He could review their needs and make suggestions of other homes they might want to see as well as the one they picked. The wife quickly replied, "Oh, we're pretty up-to-date with what's available—we've been working with a couple of different agents."

Joe felt his blood pressure rising again at the audacity of people using agents in this capacity, but he kept calm and said, "You may want to consider working with just *one* agent at a time. No agent is going to work very hard for you if they have no assurance that they will ever be paid." The woman grew quiet for a moment and then agreed to meet with Joe. But as Joe drives to the office, he can't help but feel that this relationship didn't start out on the best foot.

What he didn't say to the woman was that a couple of months ago, an agent in the next town had met "buyers" at a listed house they had called to see. The agent was held up at knife-point by thieves masquerading as homebuyers. The agent was okay, but it would be unlikely that he would recover his wallet or its contents. Joe's entire office was notified six months ago that in another scenario, a female agent had been physically attacked at a public open house. Since he heard that, Joe had been very reticent to meet people he doesn't know at empty houses. Maybe these crimes were the exception, but why take a chance?

8:01 A.M.

At his office, after exchanging pleasantries, Joe sits down with the couple and says, "Before we get started, our state requires that I review the different forms of agency at our first meeting." The husband interrupts him to say, "We know all about that agency stuff and if you're going to give us a pitch about signing an exclusive contract with you, don't waste your time. I don't know what you discussed with my wife, but the way I figure it, why have one agent working for you when you can have several?" Joe is starting to steam, but he takes a deep breath and calmly says, "Irrespective of the service, or lack thereof that you may receive, there is the issue of the agents' time. Do you understand that the only agent that is going to get paid, is the one you actually buy your house with?" The husband shrugs his shoulders, "That's the way it is in your business—it's a numbers game. I'm not getting roped into any contracts. Because if you want to know the truth, when it comes time to actually making an offer on a house, I'm going straight to the listing agent anyway. After all, they will be getting 'both sides' so I can get them to cut me a deal."

At this point, Joe is really incredulous though he has heard these half-truths from other buyers. He simply replies, "It's clear to me that we're not going to be able to work together. But for the record, you're not likely to be able to cut a deal by going to the listing agent. They represent the seller, and if anyone's going to get a break, it'll be the seller, not you." He then politely shows them out.

9:37 A.M.

He hops in the car to go to one of his listings. He's holding a broker open house and he wants to be there on time. Unlike public open houses, which, despite what the public believes, are usually a waste of time, these broker open houses are really smart to hold since statistically agents are the ones that get homes sold. Truth to tell, Joe likes broker opens because he can get honest feedback from other agents about the house that he can then bring to the seller. And, of course, Joe smiles, in this market, it's just good to have colleagues to commiserate with.

10:00 A.M.

Sure enough, at his broker open house, Joe gets a great turnout of agents. Wasn't it just a few years ago that agents were so busy, they didn't have time to preview homes? And the feedback was what he expected: nice house, but overpriced. *Way* overpriced. This isn't news to Joe, and in fact, he's already had several conversations with this seller about it. Maybe if he hears the same thing from others, the seller might reconsider. At the open house, another agent we'll call Sally Walker told Joe that yesterday she decided to talk straight with one of her sellers and to spit out the facts. "I told him your house is listed $50,000 over what the market is indicating it will sell for. From a marketing perspective, I've done everything that can be done, but no amount of marketing is going to sell a house that is so overpriced. As painful as it may be, you need to either bring your price in line with what the market is indicating or take it off the market altogether. The longer it sits on the market, the more tired it becomes." "What did the seller say?" Joe asks. Sally purses her lips. "He fired me. Can you imagine? After months of ads, mass mailings, and holding public open houses, I'm not going to get paid a dime. Forget my time, now I can't even cover my expenses. And you know what the worst thing is, Joe? He'll probably just go hire another agent and price it where I told him it should be." Joe makes a note to call his seller tonight after his other appointment about reconsidering his price, but he doesn't feel very confident that the agent feedback is going to change his mind.

11:27 A.M.

Joe drives across town to meet Linda & Dave Rodman. Regarding these buyers, Joe sometimes wonders if he's losing his touch. He has showed them *no less* than fifty homes over the last two months, but while they really enjoy looking, they never seem ready to buy anything. Joe has done a lot of research for them, sifting through the pile of homes that are available and taking them to see the best each week. He's also researched schools and neighborhoods and done several price analyses when they seem to like one home or another. While they are pleasant, they just don't seem to be in any hurry to actually buy anything. Linda is a school teacher and Dave has just finished his Masters Degree and doesn't start his new job until next month. They appear to have a lot of free time and seem to want to spend the bulk of it house hunting. Eric Fisher, one of Joe's officemates, told him last week to cut his losses; it seemed to him that Linda & Dave were probably never going to actually buy a house, that they just enjoyed the looking. "Stop throwing good money after bad, Joe," Eric said. "I know its painful, pal, but let them go." Deep down, Joe knows Eric is probably right, but he already has so many hours invested, let alone the gas! At $3.00 a gallon, Joe has already spent a fortune as a taxi driver. Maybe today, he can get them to make an offer on something. Yes, that's it, today might be the day.

12:00 P.M.

Just as he nears the first house, Joe's cell phone rings. It's Dave Rodman. "Joe, something came up at the last minute and we're not going to be able to make it. Sorry." Joe can't believe it—now he has to cancel all these appointments at the last minute. It took him close to an hour to set them up! But then as Dave continues, it only gets worse. "Hey Joe, Linda and I really appreciate all the time that you've spent with us, but I've decided not to take the job. We're not going to be moving after all. But thanks." Click. The phone goes dead. Now Joe is sick to his stomach. He's got bills to pay and the bill collectors don't seem interested in waiting until he gets a commission check. Worse, he's really worried about health coverage. As an independent contractor, he gets no benefits. His family is getting their health insurance through his wife, Stacy's, job. But now Stacy is pregnant with their second child and Joe worries whether they'll be able to keep their benefits. What if Stacy can't continue to work full time? They're already struggling to make ends meet. What are they going to do if they don't have her full-time salary?

12:07 P.M.

Joe looks at his watch. Trying to look on the bright side, Joe thinks that with the buyers canceling, at least he'll have some free time to prepare for his listing appointment later this afternoon. He has a ton of paper-work to prepare. There seems to be more and more forms to fill out for the office if he wants to get paid. All this while his checks continue to shrink. He thinks about a conversation he had last week with one of his sellers who was complaining about high commissions. The seller joked about Joe going on an extended vacation on the $20,000 the seller would be paying out when his house closed next week. "Twenty thousand?!" Joe said to the seller. "I wish!"

He went on to explain to his seller how little of that $20,000 he actually gets. First of all, half goes to his co-broke (the agent bringing the buyer). He's on a 60/40 split with his office, so even though the office gets $10,000 his check is only $6,000. After taxes, he's left with only about $4,000. That $4,000 has to not only cover the expenses of that listing but it has to cover the time spent on all the listings that never sold. And the buyers that never bought.

On top of that, he has to cover his regular costs of doing business and those costs keep growing with all of the "new and improved" technology. Joe remembered talking with some buyers last week who actually came right out and asked him if he would be willing to "rebate" to them 25 percent of his commission when they closed! Twenty-five percent?! Their reasoning was: The Internet allowed them to get addresses and do their own "drive-bys," thus lessening Joe's "work." Shouldn't they be rewarded for that?

All that wonderful technology costs money. Don't they understand that Joe is the one paying to provide that property search service that they are receiving their information from in the first place? Joe shakes his head when he thinks about when he first got into the business. All you had to do was pay your dues to the national and local boards and get some business cards. Now, to stay in business, one has to have a cell phone, a computer, a fax machine, a scanner, a website, a color printer, lock-boxes, a laptop with air card for online access on the road, a reliable car—the list goes on and on! But what really gets Joe upset again and again is that the public doesn't understand that his value is not in driving around looking at houses, it's getting them the best value once they've found it.

1:30 P.M.

Joe grabs a sandwich at a local eatery, and checks his voicemail.

3:30 P.M.

It's time for his listing appointment, so Joe gathers his materials and the market analysis that took him three hours to prepare. All of this preparation just so that he can compete for a job with three other agents that the sellers are interviewing. It's not that he doesn't think that Tom Maxwell, the seller, has a right to interview several agents—Joe knows that he's a good agent and is happy to show what he does to market homes. But for each agent to spend hours preparing an analysis on the same market seems like such as waste of time. The numbers are what they are and certainly not a good basis for choosing a listing agent!

But that afternoon, with Tom and his wife Carol, Joe is at the top of his game. He gives a wonderful presentation on his laptop of all the technology he uses to market homes, and the years of experience he brings to the job. Joe thinks they are fairly impressed and when he leaves. He might have a good shot at the listing.

5:45 P.M.

Joe stops to pick up a few groceries on his way home and as he steps in the door, his cell phone rings. It's Tom Maxwell, whose home he just left. "Joe, I was going to sleep on it, but I don't think I'm going to change my mind. You gave a great presentation, but Carol and I are going to sell the house on our own and save the commission. We just weren't sure about the price, but after getting the different analyses, especially yours, we've got a good idea. Thanks for all your help." Click.

Stacy greets him with a hug. Joe decides to do some extra work at home before dinner to get a jump on his next day.

A Decision for Consumers Rick and Sue Jones

Rick and Sue

Rick and Sue are in their early 30s with a 4-year-old son and a 1-year-old daughter. They have a decision to make. Rick was just offered a new job. The position sounds wonderful and the salary provides a nice raise. However, it's two hours away, so if he takes the job, they are going to have to move.

Rick and Sue really struggled to buy their present house two years ago. Then it was a "seller's market" with sky-high prices and five buyers for every available home. But Rick and Sue had also learned a valuable lesson—unfortunately from the disastrous experience of many of their friends—and so they hired a buyer's agent to help them buy this present home. Many of Rick and Sue's friends had "gone it alone" in buying a home. It seemed at the time that all the media could talk about was that with all the home listings online, did you need a real estate agent? Rick and Sue learned a particularly valuable lesson from their friends Bob and Liz:

Bob and Liz

Bob and Liz bought a home a year before Rick and Sue did. They both worked in the high-tech field so they were able to take advantage of the "wealth" of free online real estate information and services. They signed up on several agent property searches, and when they saw a home that looked interesting, they would drive by the house and call the agent on the sign. Of course, there were several things that Bob and Liz didn't understand. First that even though the property searches were free to them, they certainly weren't free to the agents that provided them, and in fairness, these agents should have been given the opportunity to show them homes of interest. But like a majority of the population, Bob and Liz didn't think about this, simply because they didn't know. And Bob and Liz figured that the agent on the sign was the best person to call—after all, they would know the most about this particular house, no?

Wow, did Bob and Liz get burned! They put in an offer on one of the homes with the listing agent on the sign. The agent was nice enough, but told them that there was already another offer on the house, so they better put in an overbid if they wanted it. As the current list price of the house was $372,000, they had to pay $15,000 over the list price—$387,000—in order to get the house. They found out later that the agent was pitting one buyer against the other, trying to get the highest price for their seller. The agent didn't do anything wrong—after all, the seller was their client and the agent's job was/is to work in their client's best interest. But worse for Bob and Liz, they asked the listing agent for a recommendation on a home inspector. At the time, Bob and Liz figured that they probably should check out other inspectors, but they were under so much pressure! The agent kept telling them that they better not ask for anything else because there were two other back-up offers.

After they closed on the house, they found out that the inspector missed a leak in the roof. He also failed to tell them that much of the exterior siding had rotted as well as the underlying boards from pest infestation. Bob and Liz ended up having to replace the roof and much of the siding at a cost of over $30,000. They now had $417,000 "invested" in their home. Last month, they decided to refinance and were devastated to discover that they had no equity. Not only did they overpay for the house and sink another $30,000 into it for repairs, but the market had shifted and prices were dropping. It would be years before they could financially recover from this purchase. Regardless, they had an agent do a market analysis (after all, agents are always advertising them as *free*), but they found out that if they were going to sell today, they would probably lose over $50,000.

This story gave Rick and Sue nightmares as they considered their options.

Katie and Mike

Another couple that Rick and Sue were friendly with, Katie and Mike got royally screwed on their mortgage. They went with a company that Mike found online that promised "unbelievable" rates. Because they were buying direct from a For-Sale-By-Owner, there was no one to caution them about the risks of getting a mortgage online. The mortgage field is very competitive, and since online lenders get their business from advertising, not word-of-mouth, they can offer false promises regarding rates and programs without the accountability.

Katie and Mike chose an online lender whose rates were too good to pass up and, as things happen, the problems started soon after they signed the purchase and sale agreement. They were concerned when they heard from the seller that no appraiser had called to schedule an appraisal of the property. Katie and Mike emailed the lender several times, trying to find out if the appraisal had been ordered. They were told that if the appraisal wasn't done in a timely fashion, they might not get their loan commitment by the due date. This was very serious. They risked losing their entire deposit, which in their case was 20 percent, or $77,000.

Sure enough, when the lender finally got in touch with them, he said that he was sorry, things got backed up, but he would get someone out there right away. On the day before the commitment date, the lender called Mike and Katie to tell them that he couldn't get them the promised program after all, but that they were really "lucky" because he was able to find another investor. This loan carried a much higher interest rate; higher, in fact, than the rate offered by the local lenders that had been originally recommended to them. Katie and Mike were completely frustrated, but what could they do? It was too late to bring in another lender because if they didn't make the commitment date, the sellers would be able to keep the entire deposit.

So, Katie and Mike had to accept the loan with an interest rate that was a full two points higher than what they could have gotten with a local lender. Worse, the online lender didn't even return their calls when they complained. But why should that lender somewhere out there in "dot-com-land" even care? Unlike a local lender who gets their business from referrals and real estate agents, and hopefully aims to be a respected member of the community, online lenders get theirs from advertising. If someone gets a bad deal, it doesn't hurt their reputation, they just go on to the next borrower. And the next.

Back to Rick and Sue. They had hired Marlene Brady, a buyer agent that had come recommended, to assist them in buying their first home two years ago. Marlene was great and helped them to avoid the disasters that befell their friends. Because she was working in Rick and Sue's interest, her recommended home inspector was not only efficient but also thorough. In fact, when he inspected the first house they put an offer in on, it turned out to have major structural problems and Marlene was able to get their deposit back. The second home they put an offer in on, they bought, and it happened to be a much better house, and a much better deal.

As good as Marlene was however, she couldn't help them too much on the price—housing prices were still high. Rick and Sue felt that if they waited for prices to stabilize, interest rates would have risen, negating any savings. Besides, Marlene told them that usually, as long as they stayed in the house at least five years, the market would have time to recover.

Now, only two years later, Rick and Sue faced a decision. Marlene had stayed in touch with them so there was no question of who they would call to sell their home but when she came over, she had bad news. The market was rapidly changing from a seller's market two years ago to a buyer's market now. Market time was increasing with prices moderating and even dropping. After doing a market analysis, Marlene told them honestly that the best they could hope for was to break even if they wanted to sell now. Of course, that was before commissions and when they did some calculations, they realized that even a 5 percent commission (which was lower than the going rate) was more than the equity that they had accrued.

They were honest with Marlene that while they wanted to hire her, they just couldn't afford a full commission. They asked her if there were any other options. Marlene explained that commissions were the way agents were paid and the only way to save money was to discount the commission. Yet even if she was willing to cut her commission, her company wouldn't allow it—after all, under the commission system, the company was taking all the risk and if the house didn't sell, Rick and Sue wouldn't owe any money. Besides, Marlene explained, discounting commissions doesn't work well in a slow market. When commissions are cut, they are cut not just on the listing side, but also to what could be offered to the agent bringing the buyer. And with plenty of houses to choose from, their home would be at a disadvantage.

Rick and Sue considered if there were other options they might have to save some money. They definitely did not want to try to sell their own house. They knew six people who'd tried to and only one was successful. With both of them working full time, when would they be able to show their home?

Besides, they found out that Jay, their one friend who was successful in selling his own home, wasn't so successful after all. Jay told them that playing Realtor® wasn't as easy as all the For-Sale-By-Owner websites said it was. After weeks of Sundays holding open houses, all he had to show for it was a $1000 dollars loss to advertising, with no offers. Finally a buyer came along with an offer, but it was really low. It was clear that they had deducted the same commission that he was trying to save and then some. Jay knew that he was being taken advantage of, but after five months on the market, he was tired of being tied to the house and felt that he had been misled by all those "do-it-yourself" websites. When all was said and done, he sold his own house, but ended up getting 15 percent less than what comparable homes were selling for. He could have paid an 8 percent commission and still come out way ahead! Jay told Rick and Sue that if he had it to do over again, he would definitely hire a professional agent.

Sue was also concerned about the lack of security in showing strangers their home. If they listed their house with Marlene, they could be assured that people looking at their home were real buyers; people who had qualified financially. But without an agent how would Rick and Sue know if these people were real buyers, or Jack the Ripper? With two small children, Sue was not going to take that risk.

Then one day Rick heard on the radio about a company that provided "limited service." For $500 they could pay an agent to put their listing in the Multiple Listing Service (MLS) and all they had to do was to pay the agent who brought the buyer! Rick and Sue trusted Marlene and really wanted to be able to pay her for all of her good advice, so they immediately called her and asked if her company could do the same thing.

Another disappointment. Marlene told them that this "MLS Entry Only" idea was a really poor one. She explained that the MLS was never intended to be used in this way and her experience was that even if a seller offered a competitive commission to the agent bringing the buyer, most agents wouldn't show these homes. With plenty of other homes on the market, most agents didn't want to have to deal directly with the seller and do double work since there was no listing agent. Marlene further explained that all they were buying for their $500 was twenty minutes of typing. Rick and Sue therefore, would be on their own, with no one to advise them or to help them with negotiating offers and guiding the transaction to close. She told them that her company would not participate in what was clearly a terrible deal for the sellers who tried it.

By this time, Rick and Sue were totally frustrated. They appreciated what a quality agent like Marlene brought to the table, and knew they needed and wanted professional help.

But there seemed no way to get that help for a cost they could afford. They even asked Marlene if they could try to find a buyer on their own and pay her by the hour to negotiate for them. Marlene told them no, unfortunately her company was traditional and they offered commissions as the only method of payment. While she personally would be happy to be paid in another way, her brokerage would not allow it.

Rick declined the new position offered to him. He and Sue instead decided to work hard and batten down the hatches for a few more years.

CHAPTER 3

I'm Paying You How Much?

Why Commissions are so High

Why *are* commissions so high? This is *the* constant question that we in the industry hear from consumers, more than any other question or concern. Most consumers who ask it, will tell you that it's not that they don't want to pay a reasonable amount for quality real estate services, they just want to understand what it is that they're paying for. If you as the reader have also asked this question, then I think it's time that you got a straight answer.

When you pay a real estate commission on a closed transaction, you are not simply paying for the services rendered to you on that one single transaction. If you were paying for the services themselves, you would be paying a lot less.

When you pay for real estate services by commission, the lion's share of what you are paying for is not the services themselves, but rather paying for "insurance."

In other words, you are paying a premium for a guaranteed outcome, an assurance that if you don't achieve the desired outcome, you pay nothing.

Therefore, you as the consumer, pay a premium, *but have no risk*. The agent assumes a high risk, but a high reward if successful. That's how the traditional real estate system works.

The Personal Injury Attorney

The commission system in real estate is very similar to an attorney being paid on contingency. Most people understand that if an attorney takes a high risk personal injury case, for example, there's a good chance that the attorney could put in many hours of work and never see a dime. Their services are "free" to their client unless they are successful in that case. But if they *are* successful, their reward is high—personal injury attorneys usually collect at least a third of the award.

Now suppose this attorney is successful on a particular case. If you are to just look at that one case, her "pay" would seem like an incredible amount of money for the time invested. But that large paycheck has to compensate the attorney not just for the hours put in on that one particular case, but for all the many unpaid hours on the cases that did not result in an award. In fact, if you took a personal injury attorney's gross income for a year and divided it by the *total* number of hours worked on *all* cases that year, her pay *per hour* would probably seem very reasonable for the expertise, knowledge, and experience.

Suppose that a given consumer complained about the large amount their attorney would stand to receive if they were successful in litigating their case. Suppose they were to ask their attorney to take the same high risk case, but to take less of a percentage? How would the attorney respond? If she was either not very good at her job, *or* rather desperate for business, she might take the bait and cut her contingent compensation. At the same time, she would probably cut the quality of the work and time invested in to that case, greatly diminishing the chances for success. Why? Because it is still high risk but now low reward. Who wants that?

In this situation, most attorneys with a reputation for quality work, would tell the consumer that if the attorney takes all the risk, the attorney *must* receive a high reward. Otherwise, from a pure dollars-and-cents perspective, this method of compensation is unbalanced and doesn't work.

Like the attorney being paid on a contingency, under the commission system in real estate, an agent's compensation is dependent on their achieving a favorable outcome—an outcome they can influence but not control.

The difference in the comparison however, between a real estate agent and a personal injury attorney, is that while most consumers understand the inherent risks in a personal injury case, most are not aware of the risks inherent in the daily work of an agent assisting buyers and sellers. Unless they, or someone close to them, have worked in the field, most people are not cognizant of the countless hours that agents typically put in, but are never paid for. Many consumers are under the impression that most every real estate transaction closes. Nothing could be further from the truth as was revealed in Realtor® Joe Davis' average day. To further illustrate this point, let's look at a few more examples that agents experience a lot of the time:

- Sandy and Scott Seller are ready to sell their home. Sandy's Aunt Doris is a part-time agent who lives out of the area. Sandy would like to give their listing to Aunt Doris except for one problem: Auntie doesn't know the local market and therefore doesn't know how to price their home. But Scott doesn't see it as a problem at all! After all, every time he opens the local paper, there are at least three or four agents that are advertising a "free" comparative market analysis (CMA). So, he calls three of them, tells each of them that he's going to be selling his home, and he would like them to prepare a CMA for him. Now, while those CMA's are free to Scott and Sandy, to the agents, there is nothing free about them. A high-quality CMA takes upwards of four hours to prepare, not to mention the time spent presenting them in hopes of getting the listing. And in this case, none of the agents are going to get the listing. When Aunt Doris lists the house, those three agents will then know that they've just put in a lot of work that they'll never be paid for.

- Bob and Barbara Buyer are looking to buy their first home. They do their due diligence by interviewing several agents and decide that they like Betty Buyer Agent the best. Betty smartly requires that they sign an exclusive buyer agency contract with her. She's been burned in the past by working weeks or months with buyers only to have them call on an ad and buy with someone else. This way she's protected, right? Not so fast! After months of working with Bob and Barbara, Bob gets a new job out of state. The local house search is off and even though Betty has spent many hours with Bob and Barbara, she'll never get paid for her time or expenses, such as gas.

- Sam Seller has been reading that it's a "hot" sellers market. He wasn't planning on selling his house, but figures if he can "get his price," why not? It doesn't cost him anything to try, as he knows that he only has to pay the agent if they're successful. He contacts several agents telling them that he'd like to sell his home if he can get a price of $$ (20 percent over what the current market says his home is worth). Most agents smartly turn him down. However, there are a few agents who really need the business and hope that if they take Sam's listing, they can convince him to moderate his price at a later date. Andrea Agent "wins" the listing and goes to work. She expends a lot of money on materials and advertising, and countless hours marketing the home. Sadly, Sam won't budge on his price, and after three months, decides to pull his house off the market. Andrea Agent has just spent a lot of money that she'll never be reimbursed for, and many hours that she'll never be paid for.

The previous examples are not cited in order to make you feel sorry for real estate agents, but there is a common perception that under the commission system real estate agents are all driving BMW's and vacationing in the Caribbean.

When I teach my consulting course, the Accredited Consultant in Real Estate™ (ACRE), to agents, I always ask them to do the following exercise: Take their gross commission income last year and divide by 12 so they now have their average monthly income. Then divide that income by the total number of hours they estimate they work in a month. If they can't estimate that, I tell them to break it down into a weekly figure. The sad truth is that with all that the requirements, training, liability, and continuing education, the average agent today earns less than minimum wage.

In addition, I haven't found one agent who completed this exercise that *wasn't* surprised at how little they make an hour. It's because they don't think in terms of hourly worth. When we as agents get a check, we almost always forget how many unpaid hours (and transactions that fell apart) that check has to cover before we can move forward towards profit—and our BMWs and Caribbean vacations.

Please note as well that in each of the previous examples given, the consumer did nothing wrong. Sandy, Scott, and Sam are simply taking advantage of some of the "free" services that are offered in the real estate arena. And it's certainly no fault of Bob and Barbara that they've been transferred. My point is that all those unpaid hours and un-reimbursed expenses have to be made up somewhere. And where they're made up is by the transactions that *do* successfully close.

To give you an idea how much agent time and work is never paid for, take a look at my team. Because of our unique team policies (we won't work with a buyer unless they are willing to first, take the time for a buyer consultation and work under buyer agency contract, and we rarely take overpriced listings), my team members compile far fewer unpaid hours than the average agent. Yet, last year, we closed only 20 percent of the buyers and sellers that we worked with in some capacity.

Of course, if you're like many home sellers I speak with, you may feel it's not fair to "subsidize" the consumers that use agents' time and resources, but don't ever buy or sell. I agree with you, it's not fair; and with housing prices and consumer debt having risen so fast over the last few years, a 5, 6, or 7 percent commission can often—and will—be a prohibitive cost. It's a situation that for both the agent and the consumer can often be lose/lose.

When I speak with a seller who complains that commissions are high, I do feel for them, but I am also compelled to tell them the truth. As Blanche Evans, editor of *Realty Times* explained in a recent article,

> What agents need to explain to their customers and clients is that with commissions they're paying for risk mitigation. The reason they pay a commission is to offload some or most of the risk onto the real estate agent. Those risks include making sure the paperwork is circumspect and will stand up in a dispute, protecting the home from being entered by unqualified buyers who may be more interested in raiding the medicine cabinet than buying a home, and making sure all the steps to closing are met on time and with professionalism by all parties...
>
> An important part of risk is money. If the client were to go to the bank and ask for an unsecured loan to pay for marketing their home, what would be the bank charge? Pull out a credit card. Most credit cards charge 18 percent and higher. And those are loans that have to be paid back or the bank can ruin the cardholder's credit. If an agent doesn't sell a house, they have to absorb the marketing costs and the seller pays nothing. So, is charging 6% when you have to share the money with another agent and the transaction may not close, too high?

You would think that we could put our heads together—real estate practitioners and consumers alike—and come up with some alternative types of compensation for those consumers who would like quality and full service, but who neither want, nor want to pay, a premium for the "insurance policy" that paying-by-commission provides. And wouldn't it be nice, for example, if consumers could pay a flat fee for a thorough, objective CMA if that's all they needed? Or perhaps hire a real estate professional by the hour to consult with about their real estate needs, confident that since they're being paid for their time and expertise, the agent's advice will be truly objective?

But instead of coming up with some alternative methods of compensation, many in the real estate industry have responded by cutting the amount, and quality of services offered in exchange for a discount commission. Unfortunately, the services that often get cut are the very ones that make all the difference in the bottom line of a home buying or selling transaction.

There is an alternative, and that is paying for the vital fiduciary services that make consumers money without paying for the fluff that doesn't generate a profit. How to tell the difference? It lies in what I call the "F" words: *functionary* tasks versus *fiduciary* counsel. Knowing where to put your money can save you thousands! To learn more, let's take a look at the following chapter, *What an Agent Does: Functionary Tasks versus Fiduciary Counsel.*

CHAPTER 4

What an Agent Does:

Functionary Tasks versus Fiduciary Counsel

In real estate, knowing where to put your money can save you thousands. That's because, real estate agents are not commodities, as I elaborate on in chapter 5. Different agents provide neither the same amount, nor the same quality of service.

Due to continued low barriers of entry into the field (a pet peeve of mine), almost anyone can go into real estate. You don't need a bachelor's degree; you don't even need a two-year associate's degree. Just for comparison sake, in my home state of Massachusetts, you must complete 100 classroom hours if you want to be licensed as a manicurist. If you want to be licensed as a cosmetologist, make that 1000 classroom hours. But if you want to be licensed to guide consumers in what may be the largest, and perhaps the most emotional, financial purchase or sale, you need only complete 24 hours of classroom training. *Twenty-four!* A day's worth!

Here is a joke that one of my colleagues from California told me:

I have a friend who was pulled over yesterday for speeding. The police officer asked him for his registration and real estate license. "Don't you mean my driver's license?" he asked. "No," said the officer, "I mean your real estate license. Not everyone has a driver's license."

But being good enough to stay in real estate is another matter entirely. "The turnover of new agents is tremendous," says Paul Gorney, director of agent selection at Agents Across America, an online network of real estate agents. Based on his firm's experience, he estimates that about seven of ten new agents will leave real estate to return to their former careers within two years.

And according to RealtyU® Group, the largest career development company and network of real estate schools in the country, approximately 50 percent of all new licensees leave the industry before their first anniversary.

To last in real estate and to have a productive business over the long haul, an agent must not only have the marketing, sales, and organizational skills to perform the functionary tasks needed for the job, but more importantly, they must have the expertise, knowledge, as well as the experience to be able to provide the fiduciary counsel that will make all the difference in their clients' bottom line.

If you want to get your best value when you sell a home, it's *vital* to understand the difference between functionary and fiduciary.

Functionary tasks are what most sellers think of when they they're asked what a listing agent does. They include installing a lock box or sign, taking digital photos of the exterior and interiors of the home, producing feature sheets that showcase its amenities, or installing a yard sign. These functionary tasks are important and need to be done to successfully sell a home for top dollar. Here's the catch: While they often are done more expediently by a real estate professional, some of these tasks can be done using technology, by an assistant, or by the consumer themselves. For a homeowner, functionary tasks are fabulous areas to tackle (or possibly eliminate) if you want to save money, depending on what your skills, needs, and time allow. Understand that functionary tasks should not be the reason for why you hire a listing agent.

> *A good listing agent's highest value is not in locating buyers, though it's certainly an important part of what they do. A listing agent's highest value lies in negotiating the best deal, and then troubleshooting the transaction for their seller-client once the buyer is found.*

Likewise, if you were to ask most home buyers what a buyer agent probably does for them, they would list things like doing home searches, making appointments, or running paperwork around. Again, these are functionary tasks, and while important, they can often be done by an assistant using technology. Certainly buyers can save themselves a lot of time by first doing "drive-bys" of homes that are of interest to them to learn neighborhoods and towns. But playing "tour guide" should not be the reason one hires a buyer's agent.

> *A good buyer agent's highest value is not in finding a home, though they certainly have the technology tools to do so. Their highest value is in getting the best deal for their buyer-client once the home is found.*

Here's the real news flash, folks—Some functionary tasks, such as manning a public open house (except in a rampant seller's market) are pure frill and are often only included by agents in their array of listing services as a way to justify their commission.

The Truth About Public Open Houses

You want to hear one of the best kept secrets in real estate? *Public open houses are rarely ever a cause or even instrumental in selling a house.*

In a recent article, "Is an Open House a Waste of Time?" on MSN's website, Los Angeles real estate agent, Liz Johnson states that she loves open houses, but not because they move her properties. The real reason Johnson holds them is because they bring her more business. Prospective home buyers walk through and ask what other listings she has. "They've always been better for agents than sellers," she writes. Johnson is not alone. It's common knowledge amongst real estate agents that open houses are not very effective in actually selling a house.

That doesn't mean that sales don't happen at open houses. It's just that it is likely that the sale would have occurred anyway. Most serious, qualified buyers today (the ones you want) have their own agent. And with buyer agency rapidly becoming the standard in many parts of the country, as time moves on, there will be fewer and fewer serious buyers that won't have their own agent. Represented buyers can have their agent schedule a home viewing anytime, so they don't have to wait for a public open house to see it. And sellers have the peace of mind knowing that any buyers who enter their home have been qualified by an agent and are in fact, buyers.

The truth is, public open houses usually attract one of two types of people, would-be buyers who are just starting the process and not ready or not qualified to buy or nosy neighbors who'd like to see how you decorated your home. Seriously! My mom (though she is certainly not nosy, just interested in the design and features of homes) loves open houses! If she has a Sunday afternoon available and there are interesting homes being held "open," she likes being able to see different home features while staying anonymous. I can guarantee you that she is not a buyer, but is simply someone taking advantage of a practice that has outlived its usefulness.

And why don't most agents tell the consumer the truth about public open houses?

- Most sellers expect open houses since they believe that they actually sell the homes.

- If an agent doesn't have good marketing skills, original and effective techniques for bringing listings to the attention of likely buyers, and/or the technology skills to showcase their listings online, open houses show the seller that they are at least doing something to earn their commission.

- They are an avenue of new business for the agent. Those brand new buyers will almost never buy the house that is being held open, but sometimes they can become new customers for other homes.

The biggest reason that agents don't tell the public the truth about open houses is that it's much easier to keep holding open houses every Sunday than to tell the seller what they may not want to hear, especially in a slow market. Most homes will sell for the right price, but no number of open houses are going to sell an overpriced home. Ever.

An "Opening" for Crime

But hey, if agents are okay with spending every Sunday sitting at someone's house and sellers are okay with vacating their house every Sunday, I wouldn't be as tempted to blow the cover on this outdated practice. I feel compelled to speak the truth because in today's world not everyone looking at houses are legitimate buyers or even harmless "lookie-loos" like my mom. Some "visitors" have no interest in the house itself. Their interest lies in its contents and sometimes the person (either an agent or the seller themselves) who is showing it, often alone.

Sadly, over the last few years, there have been increasing incidents nationwide of theft and/or violence against an agent or homeowner who is by themselves and showing a home—most especially at a public open house:

- In August of 2004, Colorado agent, Garland Taylor was slain during a showing of a $900,000 listing by a well-groomed and professionally dressed man who is believed to have called Taylor from a pay phone and arranged to see the luxury property.
- In November 2005, in Ventura, California, homeowner, Larry Givens was robbed during an open house by a "buyer" who came in at the same time as a group of others and stole jewelry that had been put away in a drawer while Givens was distracted showing his home to other visitors.
- In July 2006, agent Sarah Ann Walker in McKinney, Texas was presiding over an open house at a new housing development when she was stabbed 27 times.

Certainly crime can occur at a scheduled showing as well as at an open house. The difference is that if someone calls to schedule an appointment, the agent has the time and resources to qualify them, as well as to determine whether the visitor is, in fact, a buyer. But a public open house is "public." Anyone can walk in and the agent has neither the time nor the tools to verify the visitor's intentions. Think about the following scenario:

A well-dressed and friendly stranger rings the bell at an open house. As the agent shows her around, she seems taken with the home and asks to take some digital photos so her husband, who is away on business, can see the pictures online. The agent is excited that perhaps she has an interested buyer for her listing. In fact, the prospective buyer has just taken pictures of some of the seller's most valuable possessions and documented the location of the rooms. If the seller has a home security system, she may have taken a picture of the motion detectors and the security key pad in preparation for another, less well-intentioned visit.

If public open houses were a sure-fire way of selling homes, I would continue to ask homeowners to put everything of value away, take the proper safety precautions, and hope for the best. But given the poor performance of an open house in actually selling the property, is holding your home "open" worth the risk?

That is why, if a seller insists on an open house despite our warnings, my team will only hold the home open *as* a team—two of us can better keep an eye on the visitors as well as each other. If you still believe that holding your home open to strangers is worth the risk, *please be safe*. Put away your

valuables and if you are unrepresented by an
agent and holding the open house yourself, *don't
do it alone.*

Fiduciary Counsel on the other hand, *does* require the
expertise, knowledge, and experience that a quality real estate
professional brings to the table. This is what they do every day.
It's the market knowledge, judgment of price and value,
and thorough, ethical representation. It's not just the gathering
of data, but the interpreting of that data. Some examples of
fiduciary counsel on the listing side are: determining price
and positioning of a home given the market, sensing and
communicating with the seller when the market is changing,
negotiating offers for the best price and terms, and
troubleshooting the transaction to close, so it doesn't "flip,"
forcing the seller to start all over again.

It is the fiduciary counsel that gets scrimped on with the
discounters, and where the lack of this counsel causes the consumer to get burned. The importance of fiduciary counsel is
often overlooked by the seller going it alone (or with minimal
help from a discounter) where, in their zest to save money, they
end up losing far more. Sellers may shave a percentage point
from a real estate commission but they may ultimately lose, as
the lack of professional counsel will net the seller thousands
less. A seller going it alone may (and most likely will) misread
the market, not "objectively" negotiate effectively on their own
behalf (an exceedingly difficult task), pay their attorney double
for tasks that an agent could have done better (because it's
what we do), or not see the potholes that often come up
between an accepted offer and a close.

If you're going to spend money on professional
real estate assistance, put your money in the areas of fiduciary
counsel. It will pay you back countless times over. In summary,
here's the difference between functionary tasks and
fiduciary counsel.

Functionary Tasks	Fiduciary Counsel
Low Level	*High Level*
Delivers Information and Directions	Advises and Consults
Does the Task	Owns the Result
Responds to Needs and Processes Data	Anticipates Needs and Interprets Data
Tours the House	Determines the Value
Low Skill	*High Skill*
Follows Rules and Procedures	Uses Expert Judgment and Intuition
Valuable but Replaceable	*Irreplaceable*

Adapted from Keller Williams' Realty Fiduciary

But All I Want Is A Big Burger!

Imagine you live in a world where all fast food outlets worked like the real estate industry. In this world, when you drive up to the billboard menu to order, the conversation would go like this:

Billboard Voice: Welcome to Hungry Harry's! What Value Meal would you like today?

You: I don't want a whole meal, I just want a Big Burger.

Billboard Voice: We don't sell Big Burgers by themselves. We sell them as a part of a value meal: Big Burger, Super-Size Fries, Extra-Large Drink, and Apple Pie. That's the way we sell our food.

You: But I'm not that hungry and I don't want to pay that much.

Billboard Voice: Our policy is to only sell food as a meal. But, I'll tell you what—you can order our discount value meal, and we'll take two dollars off, eliminate the Big Burger since you said you're not that hungry.

You: But the Big Burger is what I really want.

Billboard Voice: I'm sorry, but we don't do it that way. And you really need to make up your mind. You're holding up the line and since we're selling so many of these discount meals, we need to take as many orders as we can. We're only allowed to give two minutes to people wanting the discount meal.

You start to think that maybe you should just go home and make your own hamburger.

But your cooking skills are lousy, you don't have the time, and meanwhile you're really hungry. At least the fries and apple pie will fill your belly.

You: OK, I guess I'll take the discount meal.

I figure by now you're seeing the parallel. Traditionally, the real estate industry has sold their services in bundles only, and when pressured by the consumer to have other options, some brokers and agents have responded by cutting their commissions and at the same time, cutting out services. Sadly, like the above example, it's the important item (the sandwich) that gets cut rather than the empty calories (fries and apple pie).

My thanks to colleague Heather Jones Taylor for the fast food analogy. The fast food chain sited above is fictional and any resemblance to an actual fast food chain is strictly coincidence.

Since consumers often don't understand why commissions are so high, many have responded by seeking out discount real estate companies or agents. As we will see in the next chapter, taking a flawed commission system and simply reducing the compensation is no bargain. Rather than cutting useless functionary tasks, these discount agencies will simply claim to give you "full service for less." But nothing comes free. What is overwhelmingly shortchanged when you pay a discount commission is the fiduciary duties, counsel, and care. These are the very things you want when hiring a professional to return the most value for your real estate dollar.

CHAPTER 5

Why a Discount Commission is no Bargain

It's Not What You Save, it's What You Keep

As smart consumers, one of the first things we learn to do when shopping for a product or service is determine whether it's

- a **commodity**, which can and should be shopped by price

OR

- a **service**, where the quality, level of expertise, talent, or experience of the practitioner can make a big difference in the outcome

Let's look at an example of both:

My two teenage boys wear "Brand X" socks. I find that "Brand X" fits the best and lasts the longest, so I stick to that brand. "Brand X" is sold in a package of three pairs and is available at a variety of outlets. Now, whether I buy this package of "Brand X" socks at the fanciest department store or at the cheapest discounter, the package of socks is the same. It's a commodity, and therefore, as a smart consumer, I shop it by price.

Let's contrast that with this scenario:

Suppose you just found out you won the lottery. After you finished your initial celebration and polished off some champagne, my guess is that the next day you would go out and hire yourself the best tax attorney you could get your hands on. And you would know that they were the best, because they wouldn't come cheap. You'd gladly pay their hefty fee because you would know that whatever they charged would be greatly eclipsed by what they would save you from Uncle Sam. That's because the tax attorney is *not* a commodity. Their expertise and experience make an enormous difference in how much of your lottery winnings go to the government, and how much will stay in your pocket.

And so it is with most service professionals. For instance, many of us have learned the hard way that when we need our house painted, it's worth the extra money to hire a painter who is known for their quality work. This is because a cheap painter isn't so cheap when you have to have the job done again. And what about using a cheap plumber who takes shortcuts which result in your bathroom flooding? Once you've had that happen, I can guarantee the next time you'll go with an experienced plumber, even if they cost more. You get what you pay for. Most of us learn fairly quickly that hiring cheap service providers is what my mom calls, "penny wise and pound foolish."

If hiring a quality painter or plumber is wise, what about more important concerns like your finances and your health? An experienced financial planner who manages your portfolio well, will make you money and not cost you money, whereas a bad one will just cost you money. Do you want the cheapest attorney if you're in legal trouble, or the cheapest dentist doing your root canal? If your child is ill, do you want to go to a newly-graduated pediatrician fresh out of medical school, or a more seasoned practitioner, knowing they will cost you more?

You might say to the previous examples, *Of course, I would hire a quality person; these are important issues to me.* Yet, often when the public looks for a mortgage lender or a real estate agent—someone to guide them in purchasing or selling their largest financial asset—the outlook often gets cloudy. Why? Maybe because so much of these professionals' value is behind the scenes, or maybe because they are usually compensated by commissions. Regardless, many consumers mistakenly believe that lenders and agents are a commodity, and therefore, shop them by price. But are they? Let's take a closer look.

First, let's look at mortgage lenders or online, do-it-yourself loans. When in need of a home loan, some consumers have been led to believe (by unscrupulous ads and other come-ons), that the best way to go about choosing a lender is to shop the one with the lowest rates or the ones who throw in the most "freebies." But there's a little secret I've learned from years of working with all kinds of lenders:

> A good lender's value is *not* in their rate claims (which change daily) or their program claims (which can change almost as often). Rather, a lender's *true* value is in the *level of service* they provide.

It's their reputation for follow through when your financial commitment is due and your deposit is at stake. It's someone who says *what they'll do* and then *does what they say*.

The mortgage field is very competitive and there are many unscrupulous operators that offer "pie-in-the-sky-deals" to get you hooked, without the accountability to stand behind it. This is why I always counsel my clients to use a local lender that's been personally referred by someone they trust or someone that I've worked with and wholeheartedly recommend.

When I hear a mortgage company spending big bucks running ads on the radio or in the newspaper week in and week out, it's a definite red flag because it means that their business is driven by advertising, and not referrals.

There are some things that are good do-it-yourself projects like planting a home garden or hanging curtains, but choosing a loan program is not one of them. The number of mortgage programs and plans skyrocketed over the last few years, due to the Internet. Some are fabulous for people with a given profile and can be financially devastating for others. Frankly, it's hard even for me to keep them all straight, and I work in a "sister" business! I would never try to figure out the best mortgage program for my own personal needs. Mortgages are simply too complicated unless you do it for a living.

Like with Realtors®, consumers are well-advised to find a good lender and *stick with them*. Why do I suggest this? Because loyalty goes a long way. If a consumer makes a commitment to get their loan from a quality lender, that lender can, and will, shop for the best loan programs among the investors with whom they work, and it will be far better than what the consumer can get from the outside.

Are lenders commodities? I don't think so, and neither should you!

Let's take a look back at Realtors®. Any agent can put a sign in your yard, or type your listing into the MLS, but as was pointed out in a previous chapter, that's not where their true value lies. The value of an experienced, savvy agent is in their knowledge, judgment, negotiating skills, and their ability to manage and troubleshoot a transaction to a successful close.

In real estate, what an agent *doesn't* know can really hurt the consumer. Let me count the ways: I'm not a lender, but I do and must have a good understanding of basic mortgage principles. I'm not a real estate attorney, but since I deal with contracts all day I must have a basic knowledge of real estate law. And I'm certainly not a home inspector, but after attending *hundreds* of home inspections over the years, I can often save my clients a lot of time by recognizing red flags in a house.

In addition, the environmental issues and regulations that I must know to advise my clients properly, are staggering: lead paint, radon, mold, carbon monoxide—you name it! And today, *everything* must be disclosed (*something you need to keep in mind if you're trying to sell your home on your own, because in most states, disclosure requirements apply to homeowners as well as agents*).

I take my duties as a fiduciary agent very seriously because ignorance of any of these issues could greatly harm my clients. My buyer and seller clients have a substantial sum of money at stake, and you can imagine that if my seller-clients didn't disclose something that they should, they (and I) could get sued.

It's hard for me to keep up with what I must know in my industry. I do it because it's what I demand of myself to better myself—and the position of my clients—as a real estate professional. I'm sure you can imagine how hard it is when you don't work in the industry. Like mortgage lending, real estate is not a good-do-it-yourself project. An experienced Realtor® who can guide you through the process of buying or selling a home is no commodity. A knowledgeable, skilled agent will not only provide peace of mind as you do whatever it is that you do, but they'll maximize your profits on your largest financial investment, *after* you pay their commission or fee. An incompetent agent is a waste of your money, no matter how cheap they are.

This is why a discount agent is no bargain. Remember, when an agent or brokerage agrees to a discount commission, they are still taking all the risks inherent in being paid on contingency, but they are now getting less reward. The only way they can make this debilitating equation work, is to make it up in volume. In other words, they will trim the sheer number and quality of their services they offer in exchange for a discounted commission. Unfortunately, what usually gets trimmed is not the fluff, but the fiduciary counsel and the personalized, hands-on care.

This means that instead of being there to guide you—the discount agent is usually running around prospecting for other discount listings.

Real World Example

Stan* is a local agent known for his discounting. He routinely cuts his commission by 1.5 to 2 percent off the going rate. It *has* worked for him in the short run—he has picked up a lot of listings, particularly from For Sale By Owners, because he offers such a great "deal." Of course, because his margins are so slim, he has to make it up in volume. He is forced into providing the most limited and functionary of listing services—typing the listing into the MLS and putting a sign in the yard.

But does he advise the sellers on necessary fix-ups and how to stage their property for a quick and profitable sale? No! Does he communicate with his sellers and provide pricing counsel as the market shifts? Forget about it! Does he return calls from other agents who have questions about the home in a timely manner? Not often! Stan has good

---

*Not his real name but a real agent in my local market

intentions, but with the deep discounts he offers that are *still* contingent on the sale, he just can't take the time.

Of course, we local agents know Stan's listings all too well—they're usually overpriced, and rarely in showing condition because Stan is going for volume and can't take the time to advise his so-called "clients." When Stan takes a reduced commission, he's not the only one who is being discounted. The compensation offered to showing agents has also been reduced, which puts his listings at a competitive disadvantage. In truth, his listings are the last ones that we agents want to show.

Sadly, Stan's discounting won't work in the long run because his sellers receive little counsel, and therefore, his properties sit on the market and end up getting far less than they should have. Many times, Stan doesn't make a dime because his listings don't sell and the sellers end up re-listing with a quality agent. Stan is earning quite a reputation which will not only drum him out of the business, but unfortunately, will smear the image of all agents, long after he's made a few bucks and gotten out of real estate.

Limited Service

No chapter on discounting would be complete without a discussion of a practice that has gained a lot of press over the last year or so. Called "MLS Entry Only," it has the consumer paying a licensee *(it's rather silly to call this person an agent since they don't represent anyone)* a non-refundable, flat fee to type their house information in to the Multiple Listing Service. This practice has been hyped up in ads (you'll see an example in chapter 7) and in real estate articles as a great way for the consumer to get exposure on the MLS at a discount.

Does it actually end up saving the consumer any money?

The Multiple Listing Service (MLS) has existed in one form or another since the 1920s and was designed as a co-operative between licensed agents. Prior to the MLS, agents could only show their own office's listings, so buyers were forced to go from office to office looking for the right house. There was no buyer representation, so buyers could only hope that an agent would call them if a listing came on that matched their needs. Sellers were at a tremendous disadvantage since their home only received exposure in the office where it was listed.

There is no question that even in today's Internet world where data is freely shared, the MLS is still a uniquely powerful marketing tool. When used by agents, the MLS brings buyers and sellers together, but more importantly, because ideally each side has representation, both buyers and sellers receive the guidance and the advocacy that allow them to get the best value when they buy or sell.

Here's the rub, the MLS was designed as a professional tool between licensed agents, not as an advertising medium for the unrepresented seller. When the MLS is used as intended, agents know that they will have a licensed "partner" on the other side that will not only provide the guidance and fiduciary counsel to their own client, but also complete the many tasks that are required on both the listing and the buyer sides.

"MLS Entry Only" listings notoriously get few showings because buyer agents know they will have to deal directly with the seller and often have to do the work on both sides, since there is no listing agent. Because of fewer showings many "Entry Only" listings do not sell, forcing the seller to then hire a full service agent and forfeit their "Entry Only" fee. Sadly, even if their home does sell, it usually does so for thousands less than it should have. The seller saved a commission, but lost far more.

Another problem with "Entry Only" listings is that many agents and their brokerages, understandably, do not want to take on the added liability of working with an unrepresented seller. For instance, my home state of Massachusetts is overwhelmingly an "agency" state. While it has just added "facilitator" to the list of real estate relationships, this status has not yet been tested in court. Until it is, a brokerage runs the risk when it places the seller's listing in the MLS, that the seller will assume that the agent is "representing" them, even if they've signed a disclosure to the contrary. Frankly, I would never want my name on a listing if I wasn't involved in negotiating and troubleshooting the transaction.

Merv Forney and his wife, Pam are affiliates of RE/MAX Renaissance and the co-founders of Choice^3 Realty (http://choice3realty.com). They represent one of the most experienced, innovative and professional real estate teams in Northern Virginia. Merv minces no words when it comes to limited service, "I am not a Limited Service agent; I will never give up the contract-to-close responsibilities because this is where the rubber meets the road, and where I can be most successful in aiding a client to close. *This* is the area where most transactions go wrong."

In chapter 4, I talked about the types of tasks that, while important do not necessarily need to be done by a licensed agent. If a seller wants to do some things themselves to try to save some money, functionary tasks are the way to go. For instance, if a seller has the time and desktop publishing software, they can certainly create their own feature sheets. If they have a digital camera, they can take their own photos and post them to a For-Sale-By-Owner website. The work may not be quite as good as an agent's since we do it all the time, but a seller doesn't risk losing big bucks.

However, when a consumer tries to play Realtor® in areas such as pricing, evaluating the market, negotiating, and most importantly, troubleshooting the transaction to close, they lose big time. These fiduciary areas are the ones for which you want to hire a professional, because they are the ones that will make all the difference in the bottom line.

This is why "MLS Entry Only" is a rip-off to the consumer. It fails precisely because it gets it backwards. Instead of hiring a real estate professional for the vital things like negotiating and troubleshooting the transaction, the seller pays for twenty minutes of typing, but is on their own, negotiating for themselves, addressing all the tasks that need to be completed for a successful close, and anticipating any potholes along the way.

In conversation with other agents, my friend and colleague, Paula Bean, who is a 26 year real estate veteran and top producing agent with Carib-Gulf Realty in central Florida (http://www.homeorlando.com), asserts that, "The biggest problem that unrepresented sellers have is with the necessary paperwork and disclosures, negotiation and representation. So what good does it do to put a seller in the MLS, when they are then left to negotiate by themselves against a professional who does it for a living?"

In her own unique (and humorous) way she states further, "If that seller is going against me, they will lose any money they ever hoped to save. I will eat their lunch and have leftovers to take home to my dog."

As a child, do you remember reading the story of the *Goose Who Laid the Golden Egg* by Richard Cummings? The goose in this story would lay a golden egg each day and the farmer was getting rich. But the farmer got greedy and one day, cut open the goose in order to get to all the eggs at once. Unfortunately, his only success was in killing the goose.

The MLS (the goose) was designed as a cooperative between licensed agents who could share information for the benefit of their clients. When used as designed, the MLS has historically been the producer of lots of golden eggs—enabling sellers and buyers both to come together in a cohesive environment through their licensed representatives. But when you try to bypass the "cooperative," there are no more golden eggs.

There are reasons that states such as Texas and Illinois are establishing minimum service standards in real estate. This is not "restraint of trade" as some press reports would have you believe. On the contrary, this is consumer protection. As Blanche Evans of *Realty Times* said in her article "Are Minimum Service Rules a Disservice to Consumers?"

> It's the nature of consumers to try to "beat the system" until costs have dropped to the point where the consumer is endangered. But it's not the nature of consumerism to look down the road and envision the end result of their downward pressure on fees. For instance, they don't see the day when air travel becomes unsafe because ticket prices have dropped so low that maintenance is cut or deferred.

Is Getting a Discount Really a Deal?

Have you ever bought day-old bread on the markdown table? The loaves look just like the fresh ones and you get a great price, but the minute you take a bite, you know exactly why it's discounted.

Unfortunately in real estate, it can be much trickier to recognize that you're being discounted where it hurts because the shortfalls of using a discounter are usually not apparent to the consumer until they are knee-deep in the transaction. By then, they often have to start all over again, not only losing the opportunity to make top dollar but also something that they can never get back—precious market time.

I have to quote my friend, Paula Bean, again because I love how she puts things, especially in her sweet southern accent. She tells me that when a seller elects to pay by commission but wants her to cut it down, she asks them what they do for a living.

As many people are paid by salary, Paula then asks, "Let's say your boss asks that you work on Saturdays for the next month. He isn't going to pay you any more for working an extra day, and on top of that, he says he will fire you if you are unwilling to work for free for the next four Saturdays. What would you say to that?"

Most sellers respond with, "Well, I guess I would have no choice, but to do it." To which Paula replies, "Now, let me ask you this. On those Saturdays, while you're working without pay when you should be spending time with your family and friends, you may be there physically, but are you going to give your boss 100 percent effort? Would you give him 50 percent?"

I very much appreciate the consumer's concern about how costly it is to get professional real estate assistance. I make no bones about it; commissions are a very expensive way to pay for real estate assistance. But if you're willing to think outside of the box, there are other options in getting quality real estate guidance that will give you real value for your money. It's not by asking an agent to discount their commission.

CHAPTER 6

Real Estate and the Internet

NOTE: I originally wrote the following chapter for a book I coauthored with my wonderful colleague, Ken Deshaies, a few years back titled: *How To Make Your Realtor® Get You the Best Deal, Massachusetts Edition.* I've added some material to it here, but the message has only grown in importance and bears repeating, now more than ever.

> Despite advertising claims to the contrary, the Internet is *not* an experienced real estate professional. It cannot consult, counsel, advise, apply knowledge of local real estate laws and market conditions, make judgments, own the result, or most importantly, understand your individual goals and needs and care about you as a client. Furthermore, while the Internet can *provide information, it cannot interpret it.*

To say there has been a revolution in technology over the last ten years could be the understatement of the year. As the Internet continues to grow from an information resource to an expedient platform for all types of commerce, it is vital to look at what technology *can* and *cannot* do. This differentiation is especially crucial when dealing with real estate, an environment where online companies increasingly clutter your inbox with ads and schemes to save you incredible amounts of money and time by using their services. One should sift through this morass of information, deals, and promises with a careful and wary eye.

I want to be very clear that, technology—and specifically the Internet—is a wonderful thing! Technology is a fabulous way to gather data and can do certain *functionary* tasks better, faster, and cheaper than any human being ever could. The danger, however, does not lie in understanding that technology, the danger is that by itself the Internet can never provide the *fiduciary* counsel required in services such as mortgage lending, law, and real estate.

Functionary/fiduciary—why do I keep using these "f" words? Simply put, it's extremely important to understand the difference between the real estate data that one can get online and the advice, counsel, and interpretation of that data that only a Realtor® can provide if you're to get the best value when you buy or sell a home.

Information *versus* Knowledge

I consider myself an Internet savvy Realtor®. In 1995, I was one of the first agents in the nation to develop a real estate website, and have never looked back. I have built my business online and continue to stay on the forefront of cutting-edge technology. I am proud to be one of only 200 Cyberstars™, an elite group of Realtors® who generate a significant portion of their business through the use of current technology. (*Of course, being on top of technology was not always something to brag about— back in the mid 1990's most agents called me the Tech-Queen and believe me, back then, it was not a compliment!*)

Over the years, my real estate team has generated a significant portion of our new business online. I'm a believer in the using of Internet technology to encourage a free flow of information from us to the consumer. And I'm not alone. You will find that a growing breed of Internet savvy Realtors®, are now offering the technology and tools that provide the most complete sources of real estate information anywhere.

I'm proud that my own team's real estate site (www.MetroWestRealty.com) has been nationally recognized over the years, for the depth of its content and yet, I've had many of my "old school" colleagues question why we freely give out so much information. They have often said, "If you give out too much information, buyers and sellers will have no reason to call you."

I flatly disagree. Although my team provides an abundance of information, we have never had a shortage of requests to retain our services. This experience is replicated nationally. The *2005 NAR Profile of Home Buyers and Sellers,* found that while 79 percent of buyers used the Internet to search for homes, 4 out of 5 of those buyers turned to a Realtor® when it was time to actually purchase a home. That's because there's a big difference between *information* and *knowledge.*

John Tuccillo states in his book, *The Eight New Rules of Real Estate,* "Information is a collection of facts or observations about reality. Knowledge is actionable." In today's information age, consumers can increasingly get all the information they want or need, but that data can be financially or personally misleading, *unless* someone with expertise can provide the knowledge in order to allow them to act on it correctly.

Information, without the context of a professional who can share the day-to-day knowledge of the industry, is just data. If a consumer were to act on it without context, they could very well reach incorrect conclusions and achieve undesirable results.

Information is like sand on a beach—it's plentiful and anyone can find it. But if you want to build a sandcastle, you may want to consult the Sandmaster who lives on the beach. They can tell you how much water to use, what weather conditions are best for building, and most importantly, when the tide comes in and how far up the beach. Without this knowledge, you could spend an entire afternoon building a great sandcastle, only to have it washed away too soon.

Myths Involving Real Estate and the Internet

As noted above, people definitely love to surf the Internet for real estate.

However, there are myths about what the Internet can and cannot do. The following are some of my favorites:

"The Internet is great! I can . . .

1. Buy a book

2. Buy an airline ticket

3. Buy or sell a house

4. Get legal advice

5. Receive a medical opinion

. . . *all* online!"

At what point in the above statements did it step over the line from fact to myth? If you said after number two, the airline ticket, give yourself a gold star!

What's the difference between the first two products and the last three services? Simple. *The first two are commodities bought mostly by price; the last three are services that require counsel, advice, knowledge, and an understanding of your individual needs.* The first two are functionary products, the last three are fiduciary services.

You can purchase the first two products entirely online and probably save money in the process. In regards to the last three services, the Internet is a great place to become educated and start your search for service providers. But if you try to "go it alone" with just the data you find online, you will very likely risk losing your shirt (or your health) if you don't consult a local provider who understands your individual needs and is accountable for their services.

Let's look at a couple of obvious examples before turning to real estate. Let's say there's an online site called weknowlaws-r-us.com. For $39.95, payable in advance by credit card, you can receive a "legal opinion." Does this opinion come from an attorney, a paralegal, or a truck driver? The site says it's from an attorney, but how do we know for sure? And what if you take this legal advice and your case turns out poorly? How do you get out of the deeper legal dilemma in which you now find yourself?

Local attorneys who are dependent on referrals for future business have a great incentive to stand behind their advice and counsel. Does whoever at weknowlaws-r-us.com out there in Dot-Com-Land care if you're unhappy with their opinion? In other words, what happens if something goes wrong?

Another example are the online mortgage companies that advertise everywhere. If you've read the business section of the paper lately, you know that many of these companies are struggling. Why is this?

First, with differing state laws and local procedures, much of the mortgage process must still be done locally, so there's little economy to doing the process online. More importantly, many consumers are finally catching on that those interest rates and financing programs are very vulnerable to scams.

Do you really think for a moment that the online mortgage company in Dot-Com-Land is particularly concerned if you're unhappy with their services? A good mortgage lender derives much of their business from local Realtors® and the community. They have to make the situation right for their clients if they want repeat business. In other words, they must be *accountable*! Not like the national dot-com mortgage company.

On a local level, you'll find that the best service providers, whether they are lenders, attorneys, or real estate agents, get the bulk of their business from referrals. You'll know who they are because they don't advertise very much. They don't have to! Conversely, be wary of service providers that spend big bucks advertising because that is usually the primary source of their business, not referrals from happy clients.

The Internet is a wonderful place to educate yourself on the mortgage process and compare different rates and programs. I suggest you take that information and the best lending packages you can find to a local, recommended lender. Ask if they can match it. If they are legitimate, either they will, or they'll tell you why they can't.

Have you ever been to a medical website? There are many wonderful sites out there for the medical consumer, such as the objective-information sites WebMD.com and MDChoice.com. If you were to visit one of these sites to become a more educated patient, and then take your questions and concerns to your doctor, that would be a smart use of the Internet. If, however, you were to visit a site and attempt to diagnose yourself, obviously that would be an unintelligent use of the Internet, with potentially disastrous results.

A Closer look at the Internet and Real Estate

As I pointed out in an earlier chapter, real estate is an interesting field in that it combines functionary tasks with fiduciary counsel. Functionary tasks, such as property searches or accessing home sales data, can be done cheaper, faster, and better by technology. And if that was the whole of real estate,

I would be the first to applaud the ever-growing number of national dot-coms promising to provide you these services without your having to leave the computer. But the problem is that many of these online services would have you believe that what you get emailed is, the same thing with the same value as what you get from a local real estate professional.

To illustrate, let's take a detailed look at home valuation companies. One or another of these websites heavily advertises that they will send you a *free* online home valuation (for an example, please see chapter 7, regarding misleading real estate ads). All you have to do is give them a street address and it's yours. So what do you get? (Drum roll please): A list of homes sold within a one-mile radius of that address. That's it.

Does this "home valuation," coming from a national site, take into account the power plant going in two blocks away from this home which will ultimately affect its value? Has it seen the home's interior to find out how it compares with others? Does it take into account the railroad tracks on the next street?

What about the local economy and the fact that young professionals are starting to move into the area, accelerating a probable increase in prices? What about sewer abatements or the newest regulations? How about the cities and towns that are developing "over-55" communities and are increasingly earmarking the town's tax money there, rather than in the schools? A national dot-com, emailing some sales data to a seller, can't advise them of any of these things, which could greatly affect the value of their property! But who can? A local Realtor® who knows their market.

More recently, a new online service called Zillow, claims to let you, *"See what an agent sees."* It was launched to great fanfare. In fact, *CNN Money* blared, during the first week of the website's launch that it was time to, "Say good-bye to appraisers and possibly real estate agents."

As it turns out, this service isn't new, but just a twist on the same old online home valuations. Meaning: plug in a property address, and *viola*, it will spit out your home's market value. This website comes with a lot of bells and whistles, such as impressive rooftop satellite photos and assigning a "value" to all the homes, whether or not they're for sale.

But are these "values" accurate? Well, sometimes you luck out and they are amazingly close and sometimes they are so far off it's laughable. Why is that? The site says it uses public data from the property's city or town. And there is the problem. Some city and towns do regular appraisals and are fairly up-to-date. Others are way behind. The accuracy of this data is further compromised because many homeowners will put additions on their home or do major upgrades without (shhhh!) telling their city or town in order to avoid having their taxes increase.

Often, tax records on recently sold properties will not reflect their true sales price. That is because the "consider-ations" in the sale are not always taken into consideration. For example, some sales include personal items that will inflate the sales price, such as large appliances or expensive window treatments. Sometimes the sales price is artificially high because the buyer is getting money back for closing costs. For all these reasons, we agents know that public records are only a starting point.

This new service however, does give the consumer an opportunity to add information, which may not be reflected in the tax data. That's helpful *if* the homeowner is truthful, objective, and has the knowledge to assign the proper values. But this can be very difficult for the average consumer. I have seen homeowners refer to an unfinished room in the basement *sans* closet and windows with leftover carpeting thrown over the cement floor as a "bedroom." Now the owners might claim to have a four-bedroom home rather than a three-bedroom. A national online service would value this home and a true four-bedroom as the same when they are clearly not.

I have seen owners put tens of thousands of dollars into adding beautiful in ground pools with cabanas in their backyards. If you plug that pool as an upgrade into a national site, it will add a lot of "value" because in some parts of the country, like Florida, a pool is a true value indeed. But up in the Northeast where I live, because of the shorter summer season, a pool is a liability to at least 50 percent of buyers.

And of course, the value of an upgrade has a lot to do with the neighborhood where it's located (more on this in Part 3). An expensive kitchen upgrade with high-end cabinetry and granite counters may be a wonderful update for a home in an upscale neighborhood, but the "value" of that remodel would be considerably less in a working-class area. If a consumer does not have a background in real estate, how would they know to value their upgraded kitchen?

Zillow refers to its website as a *"Kelly's Blue Book* for homes." I disagree with this premise. Homes are not automobiles. When new models are introduced into the market, they have an objective value with a calculated depreciation.

Homes, on the other hand, are far more unique. Where is the property situated? Is it close to the street or on a corner lot with lots of traffic? Are the expensive moldings and faux fireplace mantle really an upgrade to the majority of buyers, or so unique to that owner's taste that it may actually hurt its market value? How does an owner, without an intimate knowledge of the market, put a price on aesthetics? On a national valuation site, an ugly home with little landscaping and no curb appeal will be priced the same as one that draws buyers like bees to honey.

The above considerations are nonexistent issues for experienced Realtors®. Putting a value on homes is what we do. With knowledge of the local market and familiarity with what does and does not "sell," we can objectively look at real estate property and factor in all the "intangibles" that a national online service can't possibly do or get right.

The Internet is Evolution, Not Revolution for Realtors® Services

Ten years ago, prognosticators predicted the Internet would eliminate the need for Realtors® in the transaction.

However, a research survey conducted by the *Journal of Information Technology* stated recently in the article, "Redefining Access: Uses and Roles of Information and Communication Technologies in the U.S. Residential Real Estate Industry from 1995 to 2005,"

> Computers and the Internet have been billed as enabling new ways of doing business. The expectation was that real estate agents would go away once consumers could see all the home listing information, but that has not happened. Instead, as the amount of real estate information has exploded, it has required more professionals to be involved in supporting, understanding, and processing that information.
>
> The adoption of technology clearly has provided access to information such as listings, mortgage rates, and neighborhood demographics, previously unavailable to consumers. That increase in the quantity of available information has led to better quality information which, in turn, has led to better-informed consumers. Armed with more information, consumers have demanded more specialized services as well as better service from real estate agents.

Peter Miller, also known as OurBroker®, the author of six real estate books—including *The Common-Sense Mortgage*—and the original creator and host of America Online's Real Estate Center wrote recently in *Realty Times* about how, contrary to all predictions, the Internet has not replaced Realtors®:

According to the National Association of REAL-TORS®, 85 percent of all homes were sold through the brokerage system in 2005. Of the rest, 11 percent were FSBO (For Sale By Owner) sales; 1 percent first listed with a broker and then sold by themselves; 1 percent sold to a home buying company and 2 percent sold in "other" ways.

Ten years earlier—before the emergence of the Internet—the percentage of successful FSBOs was actually larger. NAR figures show that 81 percent of all homes were sold by brokers in 1995. That same year 15 percent were FSBO sales, 2 percent involved home buying companies and 2 percent were "other."

These results are notable because the Internet was supposed to do away with the need for brokers, or to at least reduce their role to a sort of clerical activity worth at most a few hundred dollars per transaction.

The problem with such predictions, and the reason for their failure, is that homes are not stocks, bonds or airline tickets. A hundred shares of IBM are exactly the same as any other hundred shares—it makes no difference which hundred shares you own. Houses are all different. Every property has an inherent physical nature and few buyers are willing to miss an in-person, tactile examination of a property before making the massive financial and psychological commitment real estate transactions require.

Yet companies, both online and off, continue to mislead the public about what the Internet can do and where an agent's value lies. This is bad enough when it's a third-party company trying to "cash in" by tapping into the public's "do-it-yourself" mentality, but it is particularly dangerous when it comes from a real estate brokerage that ought to know better. Following is a great example of an advertisement currently running on the radio in my local market in Boston:

> **VOICE OVER:**
>
> **The Internet has certainly changed real estate. With access to listings, buyers can do a lot of an agent's work for them. So if buyers are doing most of the work, why haven't real estate commissions come down? At Home Discount Realty, we think that if you're doing the work you should be rewarded! In fact, if you buy a home with us, our agents will rebate to you 25 percent of their commission when you close.**

To suggest that since buyers are able to educate themselves on the current housing inventory, therefore the agent is doing less and should be compensated less, is ludicrous.

While it is absolutely true that technology allows buyers to do a lot of the "winnowing down" of properties, this is *not* where the value of an experienced agent lies. As was pointed out earlier, a buyer agent's value is not in finding the home, but in getting the best deal for their buyer-clients once it is found.

Clearly, technology has saved agents from doing manual home searches and being the "gatekeeper" of information. Instead, the average agent today is spending more time than ever servicing their clients. Rather than doing manual searches and drive-bys of properties, today's buyer agent is checking out tax records and digging into the history of homes that are of interest to the buyer. Thirty years ago, it was "buyer beware," but today it is "buyer be represented," with the onus on the agent to make sure there are no "surprises."

Think about the following scenario:

A friend of yours isn't feeling well so they make an appointment with their doctor. In the time before the appointment, they go online and research all the diseases or maladies that possibly match their symptoms. Imagine them walking into the doctor's office and announcing to their doctor that since they have done so much of the "legwork" of gathering information, the doctor's job is lessened and therefore, the doctor should be paid less. Of course you can't! Your friend has honored themselves by becoming a more educated patient. And the treatment the doctor will prescribe may be easier for them because they may know what to expect. Yet they have in no way done their doctor's job for them. *That's because a good physician's value is not in gathering medical information, but in interpreting it and applying it to their individual patient's case.*

In real estate, when a home buyer becomes educated about the real estate process and the types of homes that might fit their needs, what they actually have done is help their agent to help them. To imply, as the previous voice-over ad example does, that consumers are doing the agent's job for them is simply not valid. Realtors® put in as many, if not more, hours into each transaction as they were ten years ago. Their time now is just spent differently.

While we're on the subject, I should point out that all this great technology not only fails to save a good agent any net time on a transaction, but it has greatly driven up the average agent's expenses. Truth be told, I am particularly frustrated with discount realty firms that undermine their own industry's worth in ads like these, to try to gain a competitive edge.

To add insult to injury, who do you think pays for these online property search services that are taken advantage of by consumers? They are paid for by the agents who offer them for *free* in hopes of attracting more prospects. What used to be a cutting edge application that would set an agent apart, has today become just another required expense. As real estate companies are squeezed financially, more and more of these "costs of doing business" are being passed on to the agent themselves.

One more word to the wise on ads such as the previous one: I can guarantee you that agents willing to hand back 25 percent of their compensation on a transaction that is still contingent on the sale will not be the seasoned pros that will hammer out the best deal for buyers. A quality agent knows that they are giving the consumer good value for their money. The quality of their negotiations and troubleshooting of the transaction makes that abundantly clear. An agent willing to hand back a quarter of their income is essentially saying, *My services are overpriced for what I will give you so I will give you a rebate.*

I wrote this chapter to help the real estate consumer use the Internet for what it does best—provide a place to gather information and become a more educated consumer. Again I'll say it, the Internet cannot replace an experienced Realtor®. There is lot more to successfully buying and selling a home than just viewing property listings and pursuing current sales data. Simply accessing housing inventory without interpreting it based on a buyer's needs, goals and timetable is not going to get them their best value when they buy a home, any more than an online market analysis, emailed to a seller is going to get them the best value when they sell.

CHAPTER 7

Misleading Advertising and Sensational "News" Stories:

Cutting through the Hype

Since the beginning of time, advertising has been used to sell products and services. Hopefully few advertisers downright lie, but many often mislead because they don't tell the whole story. Real estate consumers today are particularly vulnerable to half-truths since they're increasingly frustrated with the lack of flexibility in the commission model. Real estate is a field that looks deceptively simple until you're knee-deep into your transaction.

What follows are four ads, that while fictional, are based on real ones in print, radio and television. Given the money and the market time that can be lost, it's my hope that in addition to eliciting a chuckle or two, these sample ads will raise your awareness.

AD #1 in the Newspaper

We'll sell your home for only $2995! We advertise your home. We show your home to buyers. We do everything! And of course, we only get paid for results. Full Service

While Saving Money!
Contact We-Promise-You-The-World Realty 555-555-5555.

THE TRUTH: That $2995 fee does not include the Multiple Listing Service (MLS). It also does not include compensation to the agent working with the buyer. Of course, they'll tell you that's because they're marketing directly to the buyer, not to the agents.

This ad looks deceptively like straight fee-for-service except for one little detail: they only get paid for results. Sounds great, but what does it really mean to you, the consumer? You'll certainly get a sign in your front yard, but how much will they proactively advertise and promote your home for a reduced fee that they're not even assured of getting? What quality of agents work for reduced fees that are still contingent on the sale? This is known as classic discounting.

Unless it's a torrid seller's market with a tremendous shortage of inventory, your home needs to be listed on the MLS if you're going to get the exposure that ensures top dollar. Serious, qualified buyers (the ones you want) overwhelmingly work with an agent. This option doesn't bring your home to the attention of those agents.

It's also classic bait and switch. After you've had your home on the market for a month or so without MLS exposure, you're probably going to inquire if they provide MLS "for a discount." Of course they do! They will then offer you a discount commission (so much for the fee concept), but they don't take the whole hit themselves, they also discount the compensation offered to the agent bringing the buyer.

Now, it would be great if all agents were selfless souls who never looked at their compensation when showing homes, but this is one of the conundrums that today's agent faces. Few buyers have the cash available to pay their agent themselves, so agents working with buyers have to depend on the compensation offered by the listing (called a *co-broke* in real estate lingo). Yes, most agents put their buyer's interest first, but if they have a choice between a home offering the going compensation and the discount listing offering less, which home are they going to show? Surely not the discounted home.

AD #2 on the Radio

Jake: Hey, Jane, did you hear about that cool website, I-Did-Myself-In.com sponsored by We-Get-All-Our-Business-From-Ads Mortgage? Sellers can put their home on this super duper web site and pay no real estate commission!

Jane: I sure did, Jake! My friend Susie told me that she had her home listed with an agent for six months with no showings, but once she listed her home on I-Did-Myself-In.com she had an offer in one day! She saved $12,000!

Jake: Of course, if you're looking to buy or refinance, make sure you call We-Get-All-Our-Business-From-Ads Mortgage. Rates have never been lower and we're open on weekends!

THE TRUTH: *We-Get-All-Our-Business-From-Ads Mortgage* doesn't care if these homes sell or not. Their primary interest is in selling mortgages to buyers calling on the listings. Their secondary interest is in selling extras to these sellers such as yard signs, "enhanced" exposure on their website, and ads in their print magazines since the seller doesn't have a listing agent.

This ad would lead you to believe that all you have to do is list your home on their site and your house sells! If Jane's friend really had her home listed on the MLS and didn't get a showing, I can guarantee you that her home was significantly overpriced (probably because she used a discount broker), and she re-priced it to market before listing it on I-Did-Myself-In.com.

Real sellers who have used similar super-duper, go-it-alone websites will tell you a very different story. We know because not only has our team shown many of these "By

Owner" homes, but we have also assisted our buyer-clients in purchasing homes from these very sellers. Overwhelmingly, the website doesn't sell these homes, we agents do. That's because, far from saving a full commission, the sellers were only too happy to pay our fee for bringing them a qualified buyer who's been educated about the market, especially after having to play real estate agent for a few weeks (or months).

If this isn't bad enough, this particular company does a cute little bait and switch routine as well, raising deceit to a whole new level. First, they ensnare the do-it-yourself seller with ads telling them how easy selling a house is, and how with their super-duper website, they can sell directly to buyers and save the whole commission. Then, after the seller has dropped a bunch of money in buying add-ons they sell them as well as ads in the paper with no bites, they then actually instruct these sellers to mass email real estate agents, telling them about their home and inviting them to bring their buyers.

It is ironic that on most similar by-owner websites, they are very clear that agents aren't allowed to contact sellers and "harass" them, but it is okay for sellers to spam agents with their home descriptions.

Of course, after having what they do for a living belittled by these ads, we can tell you that most agents aren't chomping at the bit to show these homes unless, of course, it's a seller's market with a tremendous shortage of inventory.

By the way, I said this earlier, but it bears repeating. Legitimate mortgage companies with good reputations get the lion's share of their business from real estate professionals who recommend them to their clients because they offer great service and are accountable.. Why do you think that *We-Get-All-Our-Business-From-Ads-Mortgage* would choose to spend thousands of dollars per week running ads that alienate real estate agents by implying that their super duper website can replace them? They gave up on getting business from agents a long time ago because their service is so terrible that no agent would recommend them.

AD #3 on the Radio

My neighbors just sold their house. Boy, were they jealous when I told them that I just listed mine with ABC Discount Realty. ABC only charges $500 to put me in the Multiple Listing Service. Now, I have thousands of agents working for me!

THE TRUTH: This seller has *no one* working for them. And in all probability, they have just thrown $500 away. As was pointed out earlier, "MLS Entry Only" is a huge consumer rip-off because the MLS was not designed as an advertising medium for what is essentially For-Sale-By-Owners.

Just like with, For Sale By Owner homes, unless there is a tremendous shortage of inventory, most agents will do every-thing within their power to avoid showing these listings. Not only is there legal liability in dealing directly with the seller, but the agent is often roped into not only providing the duties to their buyers, but also doing the work of the missing listing agent. Because of the decreased exposure, even if the home sells, it will usually do so for thousands of dollars less than it should have.

AD #4 on Television

VOICE OVER: Want to find out how much your home is worth?

Don't want to deal with pushy salespeople?

*Just go to FreeHomeValue.com and a trained professional will provide a **free** analysis of what your home will sell for in today's market. It's that easy!*

THE TRUTH: There are two types of valuation services. Comparative Market Analyses (CMA's) done by computer, and those done by agents. As was discussed earlier in a chapter 6, the computer generated ones are fairly useless. This ad, on the other hand, touts the benefits of a CMA researched and prepared by an agent (hoping to get your listing because they're working for *free*). What this company is implying, of course, is that by going through them, you're not getting a "pushy salesperson," but rather a "trained professional."

Here are the facts. What you're really getting by going through this online service is an agent (or agents) who are willing to pay this outfit for leads (that's *you* when you fill out their online form). The company sets themselves up as the middle man, making their money off agents, while providing zero added value to you, the consumer.

Let's think this through logically. Who's more likely to be the pushy salesperson? The agent who *you* call, either because of their good reputation or because they were referred, or the agent(s) that calls you because they've paid big bucks for you as a lead? Who is more likely to be a quality professional? An agent who receives the majority of their business by referral? Or someone who is so desperate for business that they pay a dot-com for leads?

It should be very clear to you that I understand the consumer's desire to get honest value for their money. I know that many consumers today are looking for alternatives to an inflexible commission system, but the answer does not lie in discount brokers offering discount service, because they will cost you more in the long run. They are hucksters offering pie-in-the-sky deals and are not going to do much besides separate you from your money.

A Couple of "News" Articles

It's been said that if an untruth, no matter how outrageous, is repeated often enough, it will eventually be believed. Adolph Hitler proved that in the 1930s.

In today's society, unless we are hermits with no access to newspapers, radio, or television, we are constantly bombarded with media messages. If you hear them enough, you will, in all probability, begin to believe them. Perhaps not on a conscious level, but have you ever said to a friend, "I definitely heard that such and such is true."

If the previous sample ads are misleading, books and news articles can be even worse. We tend to believe articles that come from reputable sources, especially if they are written by an "expert." Every author writes from their own world. I always caution my two sons to not believe everything they hear and to always consider the source. We adults should do the same. We need to question what we read and ask if what the author says rings true—including the book you are reading now. Every author has their own bias.

Over the last couple of years, as a practitioner, it feels like it has been open hunting season on real estate agents. While it is certainly fair to question how the industry is structured or how it might be done better (I do quite a bit of that in this book) it is another matter entirely to take a broad swipe at an entire group of people's ethics and honesty. Throughout this book, I have clearly found fault with the traditional sales model and the myriad of discounters out there because I question whether their methods bring about the desired results. This is different than questioning a whole group's character. When it comes to big media entities going after a population of independent contractors with little or no benefits, struggling to feed their families on less than $40K per year on average, these attacks are Goliath going after David.

Many of the assertions in the following "news" articles are just flat wrong.

Freakonomics

This book which came out in 2005, revolved around the concept that economics at its base is really the study of what gives various people incentives to get what they want and need. The authors, Steven Levitt and Stephen Dubner, were heralded for using research to get at the "truth" and the book was a hit. After all, who doesn't want to know the inside scoop?

When it came to real estate, some of the conclusions drawn from the authors' "research" were not only uncomplimentary, but downright wrong. For example, the authors' claim that Realtors® behave differently when selling their own homes versus when they assist sellers. After looking at MLS data from the Chicago area, the authors noted that Realtors®' personal homes sold for 3 to 4 percent more and are on the market 10 percent longer than the average, inferring that agents are shortchanging clients.

As I pointed out in chapter 6, information by itself, without the context that someone in the field can provide, is just data and can be used to reach inaccurate conclusions. In reality, the MLS data indicated that 3.4 percent of all homes sold were Realtor® owned, yet even in the best years, only 1 percent of the workforce are Realtors®. The only way to make sense of this is to come to the conclusion that much of these Realtor®-owned properties are not primary residences but rather investments. And with investment homes, one can be more patient, which is apparently what agents, selling their own homes, were.

The authors chose to instead read sinister motives into this data. In fact, on Levitt's blog, he admitted that he "is the kind of person who is always trying to concoct some scheme to beat the system or avoid getting scammed, so I presume the people I'm studying are thinking the same way. When I think about real estate agents, I'm constantly paranoid they are trying to screw me."

Jane Bryant Quinn in *Newsweek*—"Cutting the Commissions"

My husband has a subscription to *Newsweek* and I have read Jane Bryant Quinn's financial articles for years, so I was really disappointed when I read her article, "Cutting the Commissions" in the July 13, 2005 issue. It skewered real estate agents with a multitude of faulty assertions.

She set the tone at the beginning of her article with a negative reference to the real estate "cartel" bringing to mind a bunch of filthy rich oil sheiks rather than a group of independent contractors that on average make less than minimum wage.

Her bias toward discounters and For-Sale-by-Owner (FSBO) sites is clear throughout the article. She begins by commenting on discount firms,

> If you're selling your house, a discounter can save you a ton of money. These brokers offer all the usual services and expertise. But instead of charging you 6 percent of the sales price, they take 4 percent or even 3 percent. That's a saving of $7,000 to $10,500 on a $350,000 house—a no-brainer, I'd say.

So discount brokers offer the *usual services and expertise*? As an economist, I am dismayed that Ms. Quinn doesn't see the fault lines in her argument. As was discussed earlier in this book, contrary to public opinion, the Internet does not replace what an agent does. It comes down to the fact that a discount agent willing to work for less will do less. And that "less" is the very things that will affect the seller's bottom line. As a fiduciary, a listing agent uses their expertise to get the highest price for sellers and the lowest one for buyers. The agents that do this best are paid more. The newer agents with less expertise will take less. Agents are not commodities. You get what you pay for. *That* is a no-brainer. And I'm no economist.

She goes on to laud Zip Realty's policy of offering a 20 percent rebate to buyers as a "thank you" without asking what the skill level of an agent who is willing to hand back 20 percent of their earnings while assuming all the risks inherent in working by commission. This person is going to be negotiating in your interest and fighting to get you the best deal? How much fight do they have in them when working at a discount?

Ms. Quinn goes on to cite the discount firm Foxtons which charges sellers 3 percent with 1 percent going to the agent with a buyer. She then makes the charge that, "in pre-Internet days, they might have blackballed Foxtons right out of business. No more. If their clients find a Foxtons house they like on Realtor.com, the broker can't escape showing it." Really, Ms. Quinn? And where is the proof that brokers are trying to "escape" showing a Foxton listing? If the discount model is such a great deal for consumers over the long term, it will survive. If agents provide good value for what they charge, whether it's by commission or fee, then they will prosper. That's the economics of capitalism.

Ms. Quinn continues by inferring that the real estate industry is trying to keep their listings off of the discounters' sites because the industry is anti-competitive. But no broker owes another broker access to their listings. A listing is a body of work—there are costs and liabilities in marketing a listing and that listing is usually unpaid for until it closes. One grocery chain does not owe another one the source of their excellent produce. No clothing store owes another one the sources of their clothing lines. I'm sure that Ms. Quinn would not feel she owes another writer access to her sources. The MLS is a business cooperative, not a means for one broker to get customers using another's body of work—work that does not belong to them. Ms. Quinn is an economist, and until recently I believed her to be a good one. So, why can't she understand this?

CHAPTER 8

The Unrepresented Seller

(Better Known as For-Sale-By-Owner)

Get the Facts

You might find it curious that I didn't call this chapter, *The For-Sale-By-Owner.* That's because I think "For Sale By Owner" is a confusing term. Think about it. *Anyone* who owns a property and wants to sell it, is in fact, a "For Sale By Owner." It's just a matter of how much professional assistance they want and need. The only person who can say that they have sold a home is the seller of that home, since they are the one who hold the title.

Of course, it's common for agents to say, "I sold this home" or ask another agent, "How many homes did you sell last year?" In fact, *agents do not sell homes!* Rather, agents manage the transaction and provide expert services, but even more importantly, agents afford vital counsel, representation, and advocacy.

The term "For Sale By Owner" (or FSBO, pronounced phiz-bow, for short) came about because of how the real estate industry historically has been structured, basically, all or nothing. Traditionally, if you were a homeowner wishing to sell your home, you either hired an agent for a full package of "stuff" even if you did not care if some of that "stuff" was done or if you just wanted the counsel and guidance, *or*, you went it totally alone.

Over the last few years, more choices have emerged such as discount brokers and other third party companies—both online and off—offering an array of functionary-type services at bargain basement prices, and sometimes, for *free*.

Neither the traditional real estate industry, *nor* the discounters are telling you the whole story. On one side, the traditional broker is saying that in order to get counsel and representation, you have to buy their whole package of services and you can only pay by commission. In other words, they are not telling you that some of the services you are "buying" aren't necessarily needed for your unique situation, or that you could pay in a different way and still get quality service.

On the other side, as was discussed earlier, the discounters and the myriad of third-party companies that have popped up, feeding off the "do-it-yourselfer," aren't telling you the full story either. Simply throwing your home on the MLS without any current market or pricing counsel, or having your home on their super-duper website, isn't likely going to get your home sold, and certainly not for the best value.

They also won't tell you that while today's technology can perform functionary tasks better, and cheaper than any human being, what technology cannot do is to provide the fiduciary counsel, advocacy, and day-to-day market knowledge that can make all the difference to your bottom line.

They'll continue telling you that you can *save* thousands of dollars on commissions, but they won't tell you that you can *lose* thousands more, both in the ultimate price you get for your home as well as all the other "nickel and dime" marketing costs that can quickly add up. Nor will they tell you that you can lose something else that you can never get back—your precious market time.

If you're like most home sellers I speak with, you want straight answers, plain and simple. In other words, honest value for your dollar. Paying for tasks and services you don't have the time, expertise, or desire to do, and receiving the counsel that you need, makes a lot more sense than paying a convoluted percentage of your home's sale price. Agreed?

If you are currently trying to sell your home without representation or are thinking about it, this chapter has been written for you. And though I'm an active Realtor®, *I want to be very clear. My goal is* not *to talk you out of selling your own home.* Rather, it is to make sure that you are informed about the whole process and the other options you may have, before plunking down thousands of dollars on useless services, as well as hours of your precious time on unproductive busy work.

If after looking over the information in this chapter, you believe that you are okay without professional real estate assistance—more power to you. But if you want expert help on vital fiduciary counsel as well as have flexibility as to how to pay for quality services and the caring counsel to go with it, you may want to look at the choices that professional real estate consultants offer.

You May Beat the Odds, But Know them Going In

You own a home. You know the sacrifice it takes and the rewards that it brings. It was probably the largest purchase you ever made. It is now your largest asset and, if you've owned it for more than a few years, its value has increased far faster than any other investment you've made.

It is understandable and very human to want to keep the profit you've earned. So every year, particularly in a seller's market, some homeowners decide to try to sell their home without assistance. Before you start spending serious money on ads and For-Sale-By-Owner websites and spending serious time holding numerous open houses to strangers, know first what you're up against.

The actual success rate of unrepresented sellers in selling their own homes is difficult to get a handle on because it seems that the only organization willing to put anything in writing is the National Association of Realtors® (NAR) through their annual Home Buyer and Seller Survey (more on this annual report later in this chapter).

I cannot find one FSBO company willing to give a statistic backed up by a real survey. Most will explain that it's because they are not real estate agents, and therefore are legally prohibited from taking part in the actual sales transaction of any of the properties advertised on their site. This makes it difficult for them to track how many of their properties sell and how quickly. Hmmm...this seems to be a rather interesting excuse for not providing statistics to back up their advertising claims. Is there a legal reason to stop them from commissioning a survey of the sellers using their services?

One piece of data that is backed up by a survey in writing is the Home Buyer and Seller Survey for 2005 which shows that 75 percent of For Sale By Owners end up listing with a Realtor®. It is also important to note that of the 25 percent of unrepresented sellers that are successful, 39 percent of these homes were sold to someone that the seller already knew.

These are fairly long odds, but the risk you run in trying to sell on your own is *not* whether you can beat them and be a part of the 25 percent of successful unrepresented sellers. As long as you don't spend a lot of un-refundable money trying, get help with the paperwork and other legal issues, and most importantly, take the necessary precautions to safeguard the security of your home and family, it doesn't hurt to try, particularly if you are not in any hurry to sell.

Despite long odds, however, the risk to sellers in trying to sell without assistance is *not* that they will fail to sell their own home.

The real risk to sellers is that they may succeed, but lose more than they save.

Lew Sichelman, in his syndicated article, "FSBO's (For Sale by Owners) may be LM (Losing Millions)" printed in major papers across the country in April of 2006 said,

This is The Case of the Missing 10%. It's a tale of lost millions, and it stars the thousands of owners who sell their own homes without professional help.

It seems that in their desire to save the 5% or 6% fee that real estate brokers charge for their services, *FSBO's (as in For Sale By Owners) earn 16% less than owners of comparable homes who put the transaction into the hands of an experienced agent*, according to a survey conducted by none other than the National Association of REALTORS®. (emphasis added)

Before we delve into what the above really means, let's first check out the source that Mr. Sichelman quotes, which I mentioned earlier. I'm proud to be a member of the National Association of REALTORS®, but at first glance even I would question its objectivity. Even though my team's experiences with hundreds of sellers, very much confirms this finding, as an MBA with a business mindset, I like to check out my sources.

The NAR commissions a fairly extensive survey, "The Profile of Home Buyers and Sellers" once a year. In 2005, as an example of their methodology, this survey consisted of sending an eight page questionnaire to 90,000 consumers who bought or sold a home between August 2004 and July of 2005. The survey yielded 7,813 usable responses garnering a response rate of 5.4 percent and it is my understanding that an independent firm tallies and verifies the results.

While we would all agree that the NAR survey may not be the most objective source, given its public profile, it's extremely doubtful that the NAR would risk advertising false results. Being the major trade organization that they are, if the findings were not to their liking, they simply wouldn't publicize them.

Yet there is another, more independent source. In May of 2003, *USA Today* printed the results of their study "Agents Net More," shown below.

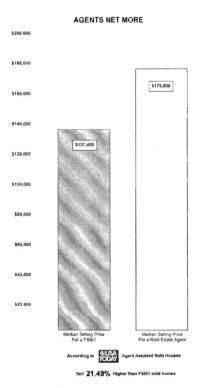

AGENTS NET MORE

According to USA TODAY, Agent Assisted Sold Houses Sell **21.49%** Higher than FSBO sold homes

The survey results were part of an article, "For Sale by Owner Can Be a Hard Sell—Agents often Worth their Weight in Commission" written by Joyce Cohen.

Still, I would prefer to confirm these numbers with surveys commissioned by the FSBO company side. But, as I pointed out earlier, although there are plenty of claims from For Sale By Owner organizations, I could not find one that could back up their claims with any hard numbers. For instance, Colby Sambrotto of ForSaleByOwner.com disputes the results of surveys showing the dollars-and-cents advantage of using a Realtor®.

"It just doesn't jibe with our experience," he says. "We haven't put together a big study," Sambrotto concedes. "But we ask all of our sellers if they were successful and 65% say they were. And we ask if they sold at or near their asking price, and 85% say they do."

With all the ad claims by various FSBO companies, it seems that not one has put their money where their mouth is and commissioned their own survey. And why not? They certainly have the bucks and the incentive, many of these For-Sale-By-Owner organizations are backed by financial entities that would like nothing better than to take over a major part of the real estate industry. If their claims of big savings are really true, it seems logical to conclude that if they had hard numbers, they would be all too happy to publicize them.

Is the reason they have not commissioned surveys because they know that the results won't back up their advertising claims?

What Does This Mean?

The *USA Today* survey shows agent assisted properties selling for *21.49 percent more than For-Sale-By-Owner homes* in 2003. In 2005, the Home Buyer and Seller Survey showed Realtor® assisted properties selling for *16 percent more*. As a seller you should be aware of these numbers before you plunk down your hard-earned money. The truth is that even though commissions can be an expensive way to pay for real estate services, you could pay a 10 percent commission and still walk away with far more in your pocket than selling on your own, not to speak of all the work you would still have to do with the energy, effort, and added liability that work entails.

A few months ago I received a call from a seller that I spoke with a few years back. She triumphantly told me that she was able to sell her home on her own and, even with paying the agent that brought her a buyer; she still saved $10,000 in commissions. I asked her what price she got for her home and she told me $350K. Here's the kicker. I know her home and neighborhood well and I'm fairly confident that had my team listed her house, we could have gotten her $400K for her home.

So she saved $10,000 in commissions but lost $50,000 in the ultimate sales price. To add insult to injury, this seller ended up paying her real estate attorney double for doing the needed tasks that a listing agent would have done. That's why when talking with sellers who are considering selling on their own, I always stress:

It's not what you *Save*, it's what you *Keep*!

As Paula Bean has often said,

Home sellers do not know what they do not know. In other words, they do not know what they have lost in price. They do not know what they have lost when negotiation time comes. They do not know what is typical and normal on home inspections, so they do not know what they have lost there. They don't know which lenders are reputable and which are not. There is really no way for them to compare what some of the FSBO companies state. I usually ask a prospective client who is balking at how much they pay me, 'What are you more concerned with? How much money you have in your pocket when this is all over or how much you want to pay me to make it happen?'

There are a myriad of reasons that Realtor®-assisted properties net far more than those being sold by their owner. They include the proper pricing and positioning of a home for the town and neighborhood, the extensive ability to market through a vast network of agents and their buyers, providing objective negotiating of price and terms, and most importantly, the expertise to troubleshoot the transaction to close.

I'm done with my warnings. My purpose is not to try to talk anyone out of selling on their own but rather to make sure that they are informed about the entire process and their odds of success before they start. In addition, as we will see in a later chapter, there are alternative ways to get the quality services and representation that will have the consumer keep more of their hard-earned money when they walk away from the closing table.

If you are still going to try selling on your own, make sure that you read Part 3 of this book—***The Four Financial Potholes:***

1. Pricing

2. Contracts, and Disclosures, and Paperwork

3. Negotiations

4. Troubleshooting the Transaction

These are *the* areas where sellers lose money when going it alone. Knowledge is power, and if you are going to sell your home on your own, watch out for where you can lose some serious cash. I'll also cover how, for short money, you can avoid them.

Please be Safe!

I wish we lived in a world where this warning was unnecessary. We don't. While I don't want to scare you, as I outlined earlier, you need to be aware that over the last few years, there's has been an increase in reports nationwide of theft and other crime, particularly at public open houses.

Because of this increase, our national and local associations have instituted major safety education and awareness programs for Realtors®. As an unrepresented seller, you're likely to be showing your home to strangers, so please make sure to safeguard your valuables and most importantly, *never* show your home alone.

Unrepresented sellers are much more vulnerable to crime because they don't have an agent who can qualify prospects. In fact, one of the greatest values of hiring a professional is to have someone who is skilled in making sure that prospective "buyers" are, in fact, legitimate buyers. When your home is listed with an agent, it will either be shown by a buyer agent who has a relationship with their buyer-clients, or an unassisted buyer will have to call the listing agent to show them the property, and it's the job of that listing agent to pre-qualify them before they ever enter your home.

If you're selling on your own, you need to be particularly diligent in requiring a pre-approval before you let someone into your home. While it's no guarantee, requiring a pre-approval is an important safeguard. Although public open houses are not particularly effective in selling them, they are a popular marketing activity for unrepresented sellers. They carry a much greater risk because, unlike private showings, you can't qualify people before they walk in. Your home is "open" to the public and anyone can come; thus placing an agent or the homeowner at great risk for theft immediately, or more likely later after being cased as well as personal attack since they are often by themselves. This is why when my team is asked to hold a public open house (and we can't talk the seller out of it), we *always* do it in pairs. Two of us can better keep an eye on the visitors as well as each other.

I'll say it again—if you're trying to sell your home on your own, you need to be cautious. Whether showing your home by appointment or particularly when holding an open house *please* be safe and *never* invite strangers into your home when you're by yourself.

PART 2:

How About Some Choices?

CHAPTER 9

What is Real Estate Consulting?

How It Differs From the Traditional Sales Approach

Let's take a look at an analogy:

The Clothing Store versus Your Own Personal Shopper

Suppose you had an upcoming trip next month and needed to buy a couple of suits. You have two choices: you can either shop at a leading clothing store or you could hire yourself a personal shopper.

If you go to the clothing store, the salesperson will probably do their best to sell you a suit. Hopefully, they will be very helpful to you by showing you the inventory that they have at their particular store. Of course, since they are working for the store, their focus is to move the merchandise. If they can please you at the same time, it's a bonus.

The salesperson is working solely on commission; therefore, they only get paid if you buy a suit *there* and *now*. If you have unique fitting needs and none of the suits at that store fit you well, the salesperson is not particularly inclined to tell you to go somewhere else. They may also not tell you that a suit you do love is going on sale next week. After all, if you come back in a week, they might not be the salesperson on the floor. This is not to say that the salesperson is not ethical. It's just that they are paid to make a sale for their store, not to find the best suits for you.

Here's another option—hiring your own personal shopper. Unlike a salesperson working for a store, your personal shopper is paid by you to find you the best suits for your needs. Since no two clients are alike, she is going to spend a lot of time upfront really listening and taking note of your lifestyle, career, timetable, size, and price range. Once the shopper does a thorough analysis of your needs, they may target one or two stores over others to get you the right suits in the timeframe that you need them, and within your budget.

Since the personal shopper knows the marketplace and the inventory, she might tell you not to buy your chosen suit right now, since they will be going on sale next week. Her goal is to use her expertise to find what is best for you. She is focused on building a long-term relationship, not just putting together a fast transaction.

In terms of paying your personal shopper, she will probably give you a variety of ways to do so.

- You can pay her by the hour
- You can pay her a flat fee to do a variety of shopping tasks

OR

- You can pay her contingent on her finding you the suits that meet your approval, but you would pay a premium for this choice since there is a risk that she will work and not ever get paid.

It's time to talk about "Real Estate Consulting." What is it? Is it some fancy new catch phrase masquerading as the same way of doing business? I can't speak for some agents who call themselves consultants yet still remain salespeople in practice, but I can tell you that *true* consulting is a totally different model—a whole new approach to real estate.

How does it compare to traditional real estate sales? How does it play out in the real world?

- **The real estate consultant is compensated for their expertise, time, and/or execution of the task. If they are paid contingent on a guaranteed outcome (the traditional commission), it is understood by the consumer that they will be paying a premium to have this guarantee.**

The real estate salesperson is only paid if and when the desired outcome (the house sale closes) is achieved. Unfortunately, for the real estate salesperson, this outcome is one that they can influence, but not control.

- **The consultant is retained and is often compensated the way other professionals providing a service or particular expertise are compensated, such as CPA's and most attorneys.**

The salesperson is compensated the way other salespeople selling a product are. (By the way, this does not mean that a consultant cannot offer commissions, if that's what is right for their client—the essence of consulting is providing choices. It is just essential that the consumer understands what it is they are paying for.)

- **Consulting covers a variety of skills and can be used to reach a variety of outcomes.**

Selling has one single focus—selling something.

- **Sometimes the best choice for a consumer is to not buy or sell at all, or not right now.**

The consultant is retained and paid to provide astute counsel to help their client to reach the right decision, based on that client's individual needs, no matter what that ultimate decision may turn out to be. A salesperson, when there is no transaction, has nothing to offer, and therefore, has no way to get paid.

It only makes sense that true consultants believe that they should first understand the consumer's needs and goals *before* suggesting options and solutions. High-pressured selling tactics have *no* place in the process of providing objective fiduciary counsel.

Once the consumer is provided with objective information about the buying or selling process and what it entails, the consultant must believe wholeheartedly that the consumer should be the one to decide what they want and how they would like to pay for it. The consultant can then decide if there is a good fit between the consumer's needs and services they offer.

If the client decides to proceed with selling or buying a home, the real estate salesperson has only one way of being paid: a contingent-on-a-sale-commission (again, the traditional method). Consultants, on the other hand, can offer a variety of compensation alternatives such as an hourly rate, a flat fee for a bundle of services, as well as the traditional commission structure, so that they can tailor their services based on what the consumer needs in order to reach their goals.

In the traditional sales model, we usually think about obtaining real estate services only when we have already made the decision to buy or sell. But in the consultative model, real estate service and counsel is not limited to just transactions.

As an example, wouldn't it be great to be able to receive (and pay for) a few hours of objective counsel on the current real estate market when you're not sure what you want to do?

So, who might be interested in real estate consulting?

- Any homeowner trying to decide whether to "move or improve."
- Any homebuyer who isn't sure they're ready to buy, but would like some guidance on the current market and the buying process.
- Any consumer, who really doesn't *want* to play Realtor®, yet feels forced to go it alone if they need to save money.
- Any consumer who has ever resorted to a discount broker or a discount commission in order to save money and found out too late that they got discount service which didn't get the job done, or didn't get it done right.

CHAPTER 10

How Fees and Hourly Compensation Work

You *Can* Save Money without Being Discounted

I hope that I have made a good case for why, in real estate, quality is essential for keeping the most money in your pocket when you ultimately close. But should that mean that you are locked into paying by commission in order to get that quality? I believe the answer is no.

Of course, after you have explored and weighed different options, based on your individual needs and comfort level, you may find, as many consumers do that a traditional commission is the best choice for you. And that's perfectly fine.

You should make that choice because it's the *best* option,
Not because it's the *only* option.

Before we review some of the different choices you may want to consider, it is important to first look at what is involved when you pay for real estate consulting services by the hour or by a flat fee.

Obtaining Real Estate Services by Fee or By the Hour

There is no question that when you pay for real estate services either by a flat fee or by the hour, you can save a lot of money. But unlike using a discount agent who agrees to cut their commission, you don't have to sacrifice the number or the quality of the services you receive. By choosing a flat fee for a bundle of services, or paying by the hour, you are receiving and paying for only the services or time received. Note that what you are *not* receiving is a guaranteed outcome, but, you also do not have to pay a premium for that guarantee—the "insurance" that if you don't achieve the desired outcome, you pay nothing. Therein lies the savings.

Paying for services by fee or by the hour isn't that radical an idea. If you think about it, fees or hourly rates are how most professionals and service providers are paid, and they're usually paid that way for a very good reason. Let's take a look at a couple of examples:

> • A couple wants to start a family, but after months of trying, they are not able to conceive. After getting a referral from the wife's doctor, they make an appointment with a fertility specialist. The couple has some tests run and after conferring with the physician, they confirm that they are a candidate for In vitro fertilization.
>
> The physician or nurse-practitioner then reviews the entire procedure with the couple as well as how the clinic will be paid—usually a flat fee for a certain number of tries. Is there a risk on the part of that couple in paying in this way? Absolutely! Because even though the clinic is

highly recommended, the couple could spend thousands of dollars without achieving a successful pregnancy. The clinic can influence, but certainly not control the outcome. *The clinic and the specialists are paid for the services rendered regardless of whether the couple achieves their goal of a successful pregnancy.*

- A businessman is quickly climbing the corporate ladder. But with the constant changes in the tax code, his taxes are getting more and more complicated and preparing them each year is very time consuming. The businessman thinks that he could save a lot of money in deductions if he hires a professional Certified Public Accountant (CPA) to prepare his taxes.

    The following week, he brings all his work stubs and receipts to a CPA who comes highly recommended by a friend. The CPA looks all the paperwork over and tells the businessman that she charges X$ per hour, and the taxes will take approximately X hours to prepare. Is there a risk on the part of the businessman in paying the CPA by the hour? Absolutely, because even though the CPA is skilled, she cannot control the outcome—the businessman could end up saving money or he could end up paying more in taxes. *The CPA is being paid for her services, time, and expertise, regardless of what the businessman ends up paying in taxes.*

- A homeowner hires a painter to remove the old wallpaper and then to paint their living room. The painter quotes the estimated material costs, his hourly rate, and the expected number of hours it will take to complete the job, and the owner agrees to the payment terms.

The painter gets started, but soon finds there are three additional layers of wallpaper underneath the visible one. In order to do the job, it will now take the painter many hours more than what was originally estimated. Was there a risk in the homeowner hiring the painter by the hour plus materials? Of course, because clearly, the painter can't control the fact that this discovery was made, and even though the homeowner could stop the work if they could not afford the additional cost, they would still have to pay the painter for the materials already expended and the hours of work already completed. *The painter is being paid for the materials expended and the work already done, regardless of the discovery of the additional necessary work.*

Real estate professionals have traditionally been paid contingent on an outcome, even though—like the clinic, the CPA, and the painter in the previous examples—no matter how skilled they are, they cannot control that outcome. The simple fact is the initial pricing of a home and the economic climate is what will determine how fast and for how much a home sells for. To illustrate, let's take a look at a couple of opposite real estate markets:

As I write this book, my local market is experiencing a shift from a crazy "seller's market" to what is rapidly becoming a "buyer's market." The seller's market that we experienced for five to seven years was characterized by a shortage of available homes and historically low interest rates that greatly increased the pool of interested buyers. During this time, it was not uncommon for a home to come on the market and within a few hours, have multiple offers. Prices escalated quickly and "days on market" were on average, extremely low. Investors were buying homes, reselling them within a year, and reaping huge profits. Homeowners could sell their own homes fairly easily, and even if they were not skilled in marketing and negotiations, as long as they could stick a sign in the yard, they could sell their home and even turn a tidy profit.

Yet, during this seller's market, the skill of an agent was still a big asset, particularly with buyers. An experienced buyer agent could often, in a multiple bid situation, "tip the scales" to their buyer by structuring an offer that would have terms favoring the seller, when all the offering prices were close.

As an example, I worked with a buyer during this time that was able to beat out the other buyers for the home they wanted even though they could not compete on price—the house was listed for $350,000 and they could only go up to $345,000. We got the house because we offered *terms* that favored the seller. This is where an agent whose practice involves representing both buyers *and* sellers has a distinct advantage over those who are exclusively listing or buyer agents. I knew from my experience as a listing agent that having their house off the market for a long period of time was a big concern for many sellers. So, we included in the offer to purchase the statement that if the seller accepted *this* offer, the home inspection would be completed within 48 hours. And since my buyers couldn't compete on price, you better believe that I included a warm and fuzzy cover letter to the sellers touting the fact that my buyers did not have a house to sell, they could put 10 percent (versus 5 percent) down, and that they would close whenever the seller wanted to.

As much as my experience and expertise could influence the outcome for my buyers, I certainly could not control it. I had no power over the fact that there were five buyers for every home and that sometimes there were bidding wars that my buyer-clients would lose. Many of my buyers during this time had to settle for a home that was less than what they wanted because there was such a great shortage of homes. *Again, while I could use my skills to influence the outcome, I could not control it.*

Fast forward to today, where my local market is quickly becoming a buyer's market. In this environment, the experience and expertise of an agent is particularly needed on the listing (seller's) side. While during a seller's market, all that needed to be done to sell a home was the basics (putting the listing in the MLS and putting a sign in the yard), selling a home in a buyer's market is a different story. This market is characterized by an abundance of available homes—often with five homes for every available buyer. Interest rates are rising so there are far fewer buyers looking. The days on market are rapidly increasing as inventory swells. Buyers can take their time, going back to see possibilities three and four times. Prices are declining and buyers can negotiate a great deal.

In a buyer's market, the skills of a listing agent can be very important in influencing whether their listing sells over the competition. It is no longer enough to rely on a sign or the MLS; now the agent's skills, particularly their proficiency in technology and the Internet becomes paramount. The visibility of an agent's website and the capability to provide virtual tours, floor plans, and town reports online, where they can be accessed by the greatest number of potential buyers, can make a big difference in that home gaining the visibility (and hopefully a sale) over the competition. In this type of buyer's market, the agent's skill in interpreting the environment and monitoring what is and isn't selling, as well as communicating with the seller in a timely manner on matters of pricing, becomes absolutely critical in influencing whether or not the home sells.

Again, as much as a listing agent's skills and proficiency can influence the results for a seller, the agent cannot control the outcome. The listing agent has no power over the fact that now homes on the market greatly exceed the number of available buyers. The agent cannot control the fact that prices are falling due to this imbalance or that interest rates are increasing. This is a market where the agent's ability to communicate honestly and with empathy with their seller is imperative because selling a home in this market comes down, ultimately, to price. Experienced agents know that every home will sell for the right price. But we also know that no amount of marketing will sell an overpriced home. *In other words, a listing agent can influence the outcome, but not control it.*

With the current traditional commission system, agents are paid as though they *could* control the outcome and that "insurance policy" of only paying if the house sells is what makes this method of compensation so expensive to the consumer.

Risk *versus* Reward

When I explain to a potential seller how they can save a lot of money by paying for the time or services of an agent, rather than the outcome, the response I often get is, *What if the agent doesn't do a good job?* By that reasoning, you would have to question whether any service provider would do a good job if their pay was not contingent on the outcome.

As an example, a dentist is paid for their services and expertise, regardless of what dental issues come up. No matter how skilled the dentist is, he cannot control whether you only need twice-a-year cleanings or an abundance of root canals, bridges or implants. He might influence your future dental health by making suggestions on the care of your teeth, but he certainly cannot control what ultimately happens with your mouth—that depends on hereditary factors and how diligently you care for your teeth. If the dentist is paid for his services regardless of what comes up, how do you know that he will do a good job? The fact is that you don't have a guarantee. That's why you usually don't pick a dentist from the phone book; it's far better to get a referral from someone who is already a content patient.

School teachers are paid a salary regardless of how many of their students ace the SATs. They are paid, and promoted, based on their teaching skills, not necessarily how many students go on to college.

And so it is with most service providers. Obviously, if you pay for someone's services by non-contingent fee or by the hour, you need to have confidence that that provider will do quality work.

Although some consumers believe that a real estate agent will work harder knowing that they will only be paid if the house sells, the reality is that top-notch Realtors®, like any other good service provider, work hard for their clients because they have a reputation for quality work that they want to protect and because they want to continue to receive a good share of their business by referral.

Smart consumers, when they need to choose any service provider, do so by asking for a referral from someone they trust who has had a good experience with that particular professional. Or, they ask the prospective provider for references to whom they can speak. If they find that the provider has done a good job for other customers, clients, or patients, there is a very good chance that they'll do a good job for you, no matter how they're paid.

Inside Tip: Choosing an Agent

When I speak with consumers who were disappointed with their last real estate agent, I first ask how they chose that agent. Nine times out of ten, they chose them based on advertising rather than by referral. I find this curious since we usually choose other service providers by asking someone we trust for a referral.

For instance, if you were to ask most people (females like me, in particular) if they would choose their hairdresser over the Internet or from an ad, most would be horrified. Why is that? Simply, their hair is important to them. So they ask a couple of friends whose haircut they like, where they go.

Would you want to put your child's health into the hands of a pediatrician based on the fact that they run a lot of ads in the yellow pages saying how good they are?

How about a mechanic to service your car? Would you want to hire someone based solely on the fact they ran a lot of ads saying, *Trust me*?

Yet some people will put their largest financial investment in the hands of a stranger whose only credential is that they dropped a whole lot of money putting their face (along with the claim that they are #1) on billboards, park benches, and shopping carts.

The best way to choose an agent is not by the production numbers they claim or the amount of advertising they do. Rather, get a referral from someone you trust. Find a friend or co-worker that has recently sold their home and ask them if they would recommend the agent that assisted them. Good, reputable agents get the majority of their business primarily by referral. Period.

Now, I want to be very clear. Paying for real estate services by non-contingent fees is not for everyone! As my mom likes to say, "That's why they make chocolate *and* vanilla." Some people are risk-aversive, and they are better off paying for real estate services by traditional commission. There is nothing wrong with that as long as they understand that they are paying a premium to have no risk. At the same time, there are a growing number of folks, once understanding that the outcome is not controlled by the agent, who are willing to forgo the guarantee and pay a lot less by fee, while still getting quality services and counsel.

CHAPTER 11

How About Some Choices?

(Yes, One of them is Traditional Commissions)

In the twelve years I have spent developing different compensation alternatives in real estate, I have often wondered why agents are overwhelmingly paid by commission with no alternatives, when the public can benefit by having choices. And the benefits are not just financial. Consider some common scenarios:

- You are thinking of doing some remodeling and wonder what improvements will get you the most money when you are ready to sell. You would clearly benefit from an agent's knowledge of your neighborhood and town, and it would be in your interest to take advantage of this knowledge before plunking down a bunch of money. In this scenario, the traditional commission system clearly does not work, since it only pays the agent for a closed transaction, not a consultation.

  As long as you are limited to two choices—commissions or nothing—you either call in someone you do not know and question how objective their advice is, or you see if you can find a friend who is an agent who will counsel you for free. Most consumers simply "wing it," based on the knowledge that they have, and hope for the best.

- Your tax bill seems to be increasing every year. You wonder if your town's assessment of your home is off, but with a full time job, who has the time to research this? A Realtor® certainly could, if there was a way you could compensate them for their time.

- While the interest rates are relatively low, you would like to refinance, but only if you have enough equity in your home. To determine this before you spend money and time on a refinance, you need to know your home's current value. Wouldn't it be great if you could pay a Realtor® a reasonable flat fee to complete a comparative market analysis (CMA) and review it with you?

- You are thinking about buying your first home but you are not sure if you can buy a home that meets your requirements given the price range that you are qualified for. If you meet with an agent, you are concerned that the agent won't be able to give you objective advice since they're only paid if you buy.

- You have outgrown your home (or your house has outgrown you) and you are facing the "move or improve" decision. How objective can you trust an agent to be in helping you make this decision, when whether they are paid for their time and effort is wholly determined by the choice you make?

There are more examples, but you get the idea. Clearly, it would make sense to have alternatives. A great example of having choices is the legal profession:

- Some areas of law such as when a client has a tricky legal problem and needs advice, lend themselves to hourly compensation.

- Some areas, such as real estate law, are usually paid by a flat fee for a task, or a group of tasks.

- As we saw earlier, some areas of law such as personal injury, where the attorney can work with a high risk that they might not get paid, is almost always paid on contingency, *but* with a high payoff if the attorney is successful.

Can we have the same choices in real estate? You bet! There is nothing written in stone that says that real estate services have to be paid by commission and commission only. Ask any real estate manager why her agents are paid by commission and the number one reason they come up with is, "That's the way we've always done it."

Merv Forney, Maryland consultant with Choice^3 Realty sums it up when he states,

> The real estate industry is very resistant to change, and it is a 'me, too' industry with a million Realtors$^®$ all doing the same thing. I decided that to compete in this arena and to seek out my client's common interests, I would have a different value proposition to offer consumers.

When looking at the three choices—an hourly rate, a flat fee, or a traditional commission—there is no right or wrong choice. As in the legal profession, different choices work in different scenarios. It's the same in real estate, where consumers have different needs and comfort levels.

Merv continues:

Based on an NAR study done back in 2000, they predicted that consulting was going to be the wave of the future. The truth is one size does not fit all, which is why at my company, Choice^3 Realty we offer three choices to our clients: traditional (percentage) commission, a fee-for-service schedule, and an hourly rate.

Currently, real estate consulting is in its nascent stage, yet growing ever more popular for the consumer. Based on this demand, this fall we are launching an online consulting course for real estate professionals that leads to the Accredited Consultant for Real Estate™ (ACRE) designation. This course will help agents to shift from sales to a consulting mindset and thus be able to develop the consulting model in their own real estate practice. I believe that both the real estate industry and the consumer are ready for change. It is my hope that you'll see Accredited Consultants for Real Estate™ in your community very soon.

In the meantime, don't be afraid to seek out good agents and ask if they (and their brokers) would be willing to offer options on how they get compensated for whatever services are required. Many agents are not aware of real estate consulting and have never thought about doing real estate in any way other way than the traditional sales model. If they seem interested, but need information, give them this book to read, or send them to our consulting site, http://www.MyREConsultants.com. There is a link on the site "For Real Estate Professionals Only" that provides an eight minute introduction on the consulting model and online course for agents. The marketplace and environment have shown that as time moves on, there will be an increasing number of agents who are either trained in the consulting model or are open to learning a new way to approach their business.

If you, as a consumer, need to sell your home, you may not have time for an agent to take the course, so speak with them about what services you need (more on this in the next chapter) and how you might like to pay for them.

Some options to consider:

1. **An hourly rate capped at a set number of hours:** This options has many different applications. It is beneficial for the consumer who would like to sit down and get some professional counsel, as well as for buyers who would prefer to pay their buyer agent themselves and have it go against the offered co-broke on the house they decide to buy.

    My favorite application of hourly compensation is for sellers who find their own buyer. Some sellers I have worked with had actually run ads, showed their own home, and found a buyer who wanted to write up an offer. If the buyer also did not have representation, they were in a situation of "the blind leading the blind." This is when many sellers would say to me, "OK, I've found my buyer, but I have no earthly idea of what to do next." Or, sometimes the seller found a buyer who was represented and that posed a worse problem of trying to negotiate against a pro who does it all the time.

    I have worked with sellers over the years that found buyers by happenstance prior to even marketing their home. At work they might have mentioned that they were thinking of selling their home, and someone said, "Hey, I've seen your home—I would like to buy it." Sometimes it is a friend or a family member who wants to buy it. In any case, this is where, for short money, you can save a ton of cash. This option makes a lot of sense for sellers who have procured their own buyer, and now need the agent to provide the negotiating and, more importantly, the troubleshooting of the transaction in order to ensure that the seller is not taken to the cleaners, there are no surprises, and that the house closes on schedule.

T o give you an idea of the savings, let's say the real estate consultant charges $150 per hour, and capped at six hours (this is our average to negotiate and troubleshoot a transaction). If it takes six hours, you would pay the consultant $900. Compare that to a commission, even a discounted commission, and you can see the savings. For $900 you have received the most important services that you can get from a skilled agent—negotiating and troubleshooting, and you have kept yourself protected. Compare this to a discounted commission which takes all tasks (including marketing tasks which you don't need), but waters down the quality. This is a situation where a commission, like a round peg going into a square hole, simply doesn't fit the seller's needs. But the hourly rate is perfect!

2. **A la carte services:** Many consultants, including my team, offer functionary marketing services and materials on an a la carte basis. Examples include digital photography, floor plan, feature packages, or a demographic report of the town to give potential buyers. While you can certainly do these things yourself, a full-time agent has the equipment, tools, and know-how to do them better and faster, and it's usually worth the cost

One very important a la carte service that you should consider asking an agent to provide is exposure of your home on their website. Many agents are willing and able to put your home on their site with the understanding that if they procure a buyer for you, you will pay their buyer-side fee. Internet presence is extremely important, especially if you are not listed on the MLS, and this is one area that sellers can't easily replicate themselves. For this, you want an agent who is not only willing, but one whose website is ranked high in the search engines so that you will get maximum exposure.

Important! *Purchasing a la carte services should be limited to functionary tasks and services!*

As we discussed earlier, limited service like MLS Entry Only is more often than not a disaster for sellers. If you want to be on the MLS, make sure that you bundle it with the negotiating and troubleshooting services of a pro.

3. **Flat fee for a bundle of services:** Unfortunately, flat fees have long been associated with limited services, primarily MLS Entry Only, which has been overwhelmingly unsuccessful for sellers. This is a shame because a flat fee, if structured to include vital fiduciary services, is a fabulous option for sellers who are willing to do without the insurance that a contingent-on-the-sale commission includes.

    And flat fee packages can be very simple. An example of a basic package includes a thorough, up-to-date CMA, assistance with completing all forms, a sign and/or lockbox, entry into the

MLS, and complete with—this is vital—negotiating and troubleshooting of the transaction. In other words, the seller takes on most functionary tasks and marketing, while paying the agent to step in and do what they do best—getting the most money for the property and troubleshooting the transaction so that it closes on time.

Flat fee packages can also be very elaborate and include everything that a seller would typically get with a commission, all except the insurance policy. My team's experience with sellers who prefer to pay a non-contingent flat fee rather than a commission, is that eight out of ten want full service. They do not have the time or the desire to "play Realtor®." What they want to forgo, is the high cost that paying for an outcome rather than the services themselves entails.

Interestingly, my team's experience with sellers is that, on average, those who chose our full-service package realized a higher sales price for their home and their home's market time was noticeably decreased. We believe the reason for this is in our full-service fee package (as well as when we provide full service by commission) we provide a full compliment of cutting-edge marketing, both online and off, and this marketing has been shown to attract more prospects and thus, better results for our sellers.

Having said that, there are plenty of packages that can be constructed to strike the middle ground—all fiduciary services plus limited functionary and marketing. The choices are only limited to what will mutually work for both you and your consultant.

The fee for various packages will vary from market to market and consultant to consultant. In our ACRE© course, we teach agents how to determine their hourly rate (better agents will charge more, but will usually be worth the added cost because of what they save their clients). We also guide them in developing various flat fee packages by determining how many hours it takes to complete various tasks, adding in material costs and a fair and reasonable profit. It is often an eye-opener to agents, who, for the first time, are coming face-to-face with their actual costs of doing business.

4. **Traditional commission:** Any discussion of choices *must* include the traditional commission option.

First of all, there are certain circumstances where paying by commission makes sense. For instance, if you are not 100 percent sure that you must sell your home, no matter what price you get, paying a non-contingent fee won't work for you. Or if you are selling a condo or a lower-priced home, you may find that you actually pay *less* by commission. This is because the costs associated with various tasks remain the same, whether they are done to market a $50,000 condo or a $500,000 home. We have found in our market that under a certain sales price, the seller actually pays less when paying by commission.

Secondly, some folks are financially conservative by nature. That's fine. Choices are all about the freedom to have alternatives. On an intellectual level, some folks may understand that the agent cannot control the outcome, but they would still prefer that the agent take the risk. If that is you, there is nothing wrong with paying by commission—as long as you understand that you will be paying more to have that "safety net."

When Paula Bean speaks to potential clients, she puts it out there plainly,

> I'm not a regular real estate agent. I'm an accredited real estate consultant. My job is to ask you some questions, see what you are trying to accomplish, so I can determine your needs, wants, and time frame. I can recommend what I think is best for you, and then, what you do is up to you.
>
> I explain to potential clients that this is how Realtors® work, here are your choices. You can have no risk and do traditional commission, but with commissions the less you pay them, the less quality you are going to get, it's that simple.

Choices. What you do is up to you.

CHAPTER 12

Determining What You Need

Seller Needs Analysis

Real estate consulting is giving you, the consumer, choices. In order to make the best choices, it's important that you first carefully (and realistically) evaluate your needs, capabilities, and the time you are able and willing to devote to the tasks required to sell your home.

With that intention, I developed a tool called the Seller Needs Analysis Form that does just that. Now, in the privacy of your home or office, you are able to spend a few minutes to review the various tasks involved in selling a home, with the purpose to determine:

1. Which ones you have the capability, time, and desire to do yourself

2. Which ones you might like a real estate professional to handle, and

3. Which ones you choose to not have done at all

Many sellers have told my team and myself that completing this analysis form (which follows) was the single best thing they did in the selling process. I highly recommend that you take a few moments and complete it before interviewing agents and certainly before you plunk down any money for real estate services. Whether you are toying with trying to sell on your own, bringing in a pro for some services, or hiring someone for the whole enchilada, it is important to proceed with your eyes open.

I must stress again the importance of being an educated consumer before you start spending money. Selling a home can look deceptively easy until you are knee-deep in the time-sensitive morass of requirements and obligations.

Paula Bean explains to her clients:

> My job is to educate. Most people think there are two or three things to do when selling a home, like you either show the house or put a sign in the yard, and then you wait for people to come and say, 'I want to buy it.' But the first question I always ask when working with a new client is, 'Why are you selling?' because everything that follows is based on their answer.

The power in completing this analysis first is it will give you a clear picture of the most important tasks that need to be completed in order to sell your home for the best value. It will help to determine where your needs may lie. You will be evermore confident that tasks or expertise that you might not have thought about, won't sneak up and bite you later in the process.

And, if and when you decide to interview agents, you can determine their level of expertise and knowledge on the very items that you most need them for.

Analysis Form

On the analysis form that follows, you will find a list of the major tasks and services that are performed in order to sell a home. For each task or service, you can select the appropriate response. As you review each of the tasks, make sure you are realistic about what you are *able* and *willing* to do. Remember, unless selling homes is your full time job, selling a home can be a huge time consumer.

Note: On some tasks or services you will notice an F which stands for Fiduciary.

A fiduciary task or service involves interpreting information and calling on experience and expertise to make judgments regarding the real estate market. As I've stated before, it involves representation of the client and negotiations on their behalf. Fiduciary involves expert judgment and intuition; it advises and consults. It is high level and high skill, but also accepts high responsibility. This is where the home seller going it alone loses the most, it is prudent to hire a real estate professional for these tasks and services.

Seller Needs Analysis

Seller Needs Analysis Task or Service	I have the capability, time, & desire to perform this task myself.	I'd like this task/ service in the hands of a real estate professional.	I'm OK with this task/ service NOT being done.	I need more information on this task before making a determination
F Research comparable active, pending, and sold properties to obtain an accurate market value for my home *(Fiduciary refers to gaining an understanding of current market conditions and how to best position your home for a quick and profitable sale).*	☐	☐	☐	☐
F Completion (and review if necessary) of all contracts, disclosures, and paperwork *(Fiduciary refers to the fact that in many states you are required to have a knowledge of what needs to be disclosed as well as your responsibilities regarding environmental regulations).*	☐	☐	N/A	☐
Take and edit digital photos of my home.	☐	☐	☐	☐
Take room measurements, prepare a floor plan (if desired), and determine square footage.	☐	☐	☐	☐
Gather city/town information and services for prospective buyers.	☐	☐	☐	☐
Prepare Feature Packages.	☐	☐	☐	☐
Prepare and post picture(s) and description of my home where it's likely to be found by online buyers.	☐	☐	☐	☐
Prepare and post a Virtual Tour of my home where it's likely to be found by online buyers.	☐	☐	☐	☐
F Enter listing on MLS *(Fiduciary refers to the fact that in many states entering a listing can imply representation).*	N/A	☐	☐	☐
Install a yard sign and/or lock box.	☐	☐	☐	☐
Hold a Broker Open House.	N/A	☐	☐	☐
Hold a Public Open House.	☐	☐	☐	☐
Write and place print advertisements.	☐	☐	☐	☐
Schedule agent showings of home.	☐	☐	N/A	☐
Pre-qualify, schedule and conduct showings for unassisted buyers.	☐	☐	N/A	☐
Make follow up calls to agents & unassisted buyers for feedback on showings.	☐	☐	☐	☐
F Negotiate any offers. Solid negotiations involve knowledge of terms as well as price. You should have a good understanding of the timing involved in the transaction and the buyer's loan commitment what needs to be disclosed and what contingencies are not in your best interest. You also need to be able to stay objective. *(Definitely fiduciary: This is absolutely where sellers going it alone give the store away. If you are going to hire a pro for just one thing - this is it!).*	☐	☐	N/A	☐
Attend home inspection.	☐	☐	☐	☐
Supply initial draft of Purchase & Sale.	☐	☐	☐	☐
F Troubleshoot and coordinate all necessary steps for a successful closing *(Fiduciary as to anticipating and dealing with the inevitable potholes along the way).*	☐	☐	N/A	☐
Attend Closing.	☐	☐	N/A	☐

PART 3:

The Four Financial Potholes

CHAPTER 13

Pricing Your Home to Sell for the Highest Value

There are some facts you should be aware of if you wish to get top dollar for your home. Let's look at the *three big questions* we get from consumers regarding pricing:

1. "What price can I get?"
2. "How long will it take?"
3. "Who determines price anyway?"

In other words..."*I need the straight scoop on pricing!*"

There is a big difference between a listing price, which the seller determines and a selling price, which is controlled by the market. *Or to put it another way*, the seller sets the price—ultimately the buyer determines the value.

In addition, there are certain things that *do* and *do not* affect value:

Things That *Don't* Effect Value

- **Your original cost:** One of the things that buyers consistently ask when they are interested in a home is, "What did the seller pay when they bought the house?" as though that would be a factor in what they should offer. The answer is, *it doesn't matter!* You may have paid top dollar to buy your home few years back in a seller's market when prices were sky-high. You may have scored a great deal because you bought in a buyer's market. But what you paid when you bought has absolutely no bearing on what you can ask today.

- **The cost to rebuild today:** Building costs will go up and they will go down. They have nothing to do with market value.

- **Money spent on certain *not-the-best-for-resale* Improvements:** There is a mantra that I constantly repeat to would-be sellers, *"What you put into your home is not necessarily what you will get out of it."* Remodeling a bath will return 102 percent of your investment, but building a home office will only get you 72 percent back.* It doesn't mean that you shouldn't make your home what you want—there is something to be said for personal enjoyment. But don't expect an automatic dollar-for-dollar return. It doesn't work that way.

- **Personal attachment:** That huge built-in that takes up half of your living room may hold many memories for you because of what it showcased through the years, but has no bearing on its value to a potential buyer.

Things That *do* Effect Value

- **Market value**: The price that will bring a sale between a willing buyer and a willing seller. It is

---

* NAR 2005 *Cost vs. Value Report*

based on the history of similar properties recently sold in the area.

- **Regression and progression**: The effect that surrounding home sizes have on the value of a subject property. *Regression* is the decrease in value of a more expensive home when surrounded by smaller homes. For example, a homeowner may have added a second story to his ranch-style home years ago to accommodate his large family. However, if all of the other homes on his street have remained one-story ranches, his two-story would *regress* in value as compared to the smaller homes.

    Progression is the increase in value of a less expensive home when surrounded by larger homes. For example, if a neighborhood of small homes all expanded over the years except for one, that smaller home would *progress* in value as compared to the larger ones.

- **Substitution**: The actual value of an amenity. *Value is determined not by the cost invested in a property, but by the value derived from it.* For example, let's say you have two identical homes and both need a well. "House A" puts in a well for $9,000. "House B" hits rock and the cost for their well is $17,000. The market value of both homes would still be the same. The home with the more expensive well is worth no more because the value is in the water, not the cost of obtaining it.

- **Investment in good resale improvements:** The best return on investment in 2005 was a mid-range bath remodel (102 percent) followed by a minor kitchen remodel (98 percent).*

* NAR 2005 *Cost vs. Value Report*

The Top 10 Most Frequently Heard Pricing Comments from Sellers

Which, truth be told, have no actual bearing on correctly pricing a home. Sorry.

1. "Our home is so much nicer than those other houses."
2. "Well, my cousin, who is an agent, said it was worth a lot more."
3. "People always offer less than asking price."
4. "We can always come down on our price."
5. "We simply have to get that much out of our home."
6. "My neighbor was able to get his price."
7. "We are going to try it at our price for a month or so."
8. "But look at all of the nice upgrades we put in."
9. "The buyers can always make an offer."
10. "We paid more when we bought it."

The Importance of Pricing it Right...

A well-priced listing is the most important factor in marketing your property for the greatest value. Nothing, I repeat nothing, can touch this. Naturally, listing a property too low will preclude the opportunity for getting top dollar. On the other hand, setting the price too high discourages showings and tends to eliminate the most likely buyers from viewing your property.

...From the Beginning!

Pricing your home correctly in the beginning will net you more.

Here are some interesting statistics:

Average Difference Between Original List Price and Selling Price by Length of Time on Market	
2.9%	Less Than 4 Weeks
4.8%	4-12 Weeks
6.4%	13-24 Weeks
9.1%	More Than 24 Weeks
	* Based on NAR Home Buying & Selling Survey– 2004

* Based on NAR Home Buying & Selling Survey - 2004

One of the top 10 pricing comments cited above is, "Let's try it at our price for a month or so." The problem with this logic is that the longer a home is on the market, the less it will ultimately get. If your home is listed too high in that crucial first couple of weeks, you lose your best opportunity to sell for close to market value.

History of an Overpriced Home

	MONTH 1	MONTH 2	MONTH 3	MONTH 4	MONTH 5	MONTH 6
LIST PRICE: $280,000	⌂					
REDUCED TO: $270,000		⌂				
REDUCED TO: $260,000			⌂			
REDUCED TO: $250,000	(This is the actual market value)			⌂	⌂	
SOLD AT: $230,000						⌂

FINALLY SOLD!

A few years back, one of my team members, Dina Raneri, went on a listing appointment. After carefully reviewing the sales comparables, she recommended to the sellers a list price of $250,000 which was what the market indicated the sale price would be and would enable them to sell their home within a 30 day market time. Dina explained that if the home is priced to the market from the beginning, it will usually sell for very close to list and perhaps even more, since there was a shortage of homes at $250,000 or less.

The sellers, however, insisted on listing at $280,000. They then began a process of what we call "chasing the market" i.e. dropping the price month in and out to try to get an offer. Unfortunately, by the time an overpriced home is finally reduced to the market value it originally was, it is too "aged" for buyers to offer full price.

Have you ever asked how long a home has been on the market? What conclusions do you draw?

As you can see, in the above table, Dina's sellers paid dearly for overpricing their home: instead of selling for $250,000 or more in a month of market time, they ended up with six months on the market, selling their home for only $230,000!

"But We Have Time!"

% OVER MARKET	MONTH 1	MONTH 2	MONTH 3	MONTH 4	MONTH 5	MONTH 6
20%				STILL THERE	STILL THERE	STILL THERE
15%			SOLD			
10%		SOLD		An Overpriced Home Will Sit on the Market UNSOLD No Matter How Long You Wait.		
5%	SOLD					
PRICED TO MARKET	SOLD			In Fact, the Longer a Home Sits on the Market, the Faster the Value Spirals Downward.		

At some percentage above the market, no reasonable amount of time will produce a sale.

"Couldn't We Try My Price For a Few Weeks?"

	WEEK 1	WEEK 2	WEEK 3	WEEK 4	WEEK 5	WEEK 6
A C T I V I T Y						

The majority of prospect activity on a new listing occurs in the first two weeks it is on the market. This happens because buyer agents maintain an inventory of active prospects that have been cultivated over time. When a home is newly listed, agents arrange for these buyers to see it. Once this active group has seen the property, showing activity decreases to only those buyers new to the market. For this reason it is very important that sellers have their home in the best condition and at the best price at first exposure to the market.

Overpricing is a Very Human Thing to Do

It is natural to try to get as much as possible for your property. It is natural to think your home will be the exception to the rule. We all hope that we will find the one buyer who will fall desperately in love with our house, and pay our price. It is also natural to reason that you can drop your price later. But while these thoughts are human nature—they simply ignore the realities of the market.

> **Overpricing...**
> ...reduces agent activity
> ...reduces advertising response
> ...loses interested buyers
> ...attracts the wrong prospects
> ...eliminates offers
> ...helps sell the competition

...extends market time

...causes appraisal problems

If you have hired a professional to assist you in selling your home, one of the first and most important things they will do is to prepare an analysis of the market and use their knowledge and expertise to arrive at a range that your home will likely sell for. Hopefully, you have hired this agent because they were a referral from a friend or family member and you trust what they say. If this is the case, do yourself a favor and *listen to them.*

Believe me, putting a price on a home is one of the hardest jobs of a listing agent, not because the price range is hard to come by. The "actives," "under agreements," and "solds" —that are crucial to evaluating and understanding the market—are right at our fingertips. Rather, telling a home-owner, who may have put years of love into her home, that it may not sell for what she thinks it's "worth" is the hard part.

A real estate professional who has a reputation for quality work will be firm and tell you what the market is showing, even if it's not what you want to hear. And by doing so, they take the risk of losing your listing, even though they are being true and ethical. Unfortunately, many sellers continue the erroneous practice of choosing an agent based on who gives them the best price.

The facts are, the *market* determines the price for which your home will sell, not the agent, or the agent's company. The agent's marketing can certainly influence in a seller's favor, but it can *never* control when your home will sell and for how much.

Please note, though, that this is not to say that marketing is not important because a listing agent's job is to bring your home to the attention of the greatest number of qualified buyers. Their experience, expertise, and guidance are what will make the difference in your profitability when you walk away from the closing table.

Unfortunately, as continuously happens, agents who are desperate for business will tell consumers whatever price range is necessary to obtain the listing. In the business we call this, "buying a listing." This practice is unethical, and negatively affects reputable agents, real estate as a whole, and the consumer. These unscrupulous agents are a waste of your time because invariably, once they get your signature on a contract and their sign in your yard, they will begin "talking you down." And by then, you've lost your opportunity to capitalize on the market and get top dollar.

I continually stress to buyers, as well as sellers, to be diligent and take care to spend time with and interview an agent before they put their largest financial investment into that person's hands. At the end of the day, the home searching or marketing an agent does (or does not do) might be important, but the counsel they provide throughout the transaction is critical. *That counsel is only helpful if you listen to it.*

There are three questions that every educated consumer should ask themselves about a potential agent:

1. "Am I confident that this agent is knowledgeable?"
2. "Do I have a level of trust in what they say?" *and most importantly,*
3. "Am I confident that they are working in my best interest?"

If the answer to these questions is yes, then listen to what they say. Their counsel, based on their expertise and experience, is their greatest value.

Selling Your Home in a Buyer's Market

As I mentioned earlier, my home state of Massachusetts is currently and rapidly changing from a seller's market to a buyer's market. Market time has greatly increased as inventory has shot up because *real estate is cyclical—what goes up, even-*

tually comes down. This change has been difficult for sellers to adjust to. During the previous eight years, sellers had become accustomed to incredible appreciation of homes.

To give you an idea, in Ashland Massachusetts* (one of fifty towns that my team covers), the average closing price for a three bedroom home in 1997 was $187,478. By the end of 2005, the average three-bedroom home sold for $381,586—an appreciation of 51 percent in eight years!

But so far in 2006, that average three-bedroom home in Ashland is selling for $376,016 which wouldn't be a bad decrease, but market time has shot up to 110 days from a low of 23 days in 2000. Nothing lasts forever and one of the reasons that houses are not moving as they should this year is that they are priced too high for the market as it is—not as it was. Sellers are largely in denial and sadly, many of them are not listening to the one person who knows the market best—their Realtor®.

I can certainly understand how tough this is. My team makes it a point to be very direct with our sellers in this situation, particularly when their homes have been on the market for some time. It takes a combination of candor and empathy to speak clearly to folks with unrealistic expectations, yet if you're truly working in your client's best interest, it is imperative to be direct and honest in a market such as this. What I, or my partner, Lisa usually say to these sellers is:

> Your home has been on the market for X number of weeks and clearly the market has spoken. Your price is too high. We have done everything that can be done as far as marketing is concerned, but no amount of marketing will help an overpriced home to sell. We have examined the market and we believe that your home will likely sell for $X–$X. So, you have a choice to make. What will it be?

*Sales Data From MLS Property Information Network—1997-2006

If that price range works for you, we need to lower your price to that range so we can get your home sold and you can get on with your life.

If you feel that you cannot afford to sell your home for the price the market is demanding, then this is not the right time to sell your home. It does you no good to have it sit and collect market time. Unfortunately, the price that you want or need has no bearing on what your home can sell for. In real estate, the market is a very objective barometer, and wishing something doesn't just make it so.

The "Wiggle Room" Myth

Before ending this chapter, I would like to disprove the myth that is often believed by buyers as well as sellers: you must build "wiggle room" into an offer (buyers) or an asking price (sellers). I believe this practice is counter-productive. Let me tell you why. But first, this is why it is important to have a buyer or a listing agent whose judgment and word you trust.

Let's look at buying. When I work with a buyer who develops an interest in a particular home, the first thing I do is run a comparative market analysis (CMA) for them on that particular subject property. You may be thinking, why run a CMA for a buyer? Know now that CMA's are not just for sellers. Running a CMA for a buyer is the *best* way to avoid overpaying for a home.

If the property is priced too high—based on the CMA and my experience—we will certainly make an offer based on what the market is saying. But my team members have all had experiences with buyers that, even when we tell them that the property is priced fairly or are even under-priced, still want to "low-ball" their initial offer. I will tell you that if a property is priced to the market, there is nothing wrong with offering close to list price, but then holding to that price.

My team member, Yolanda Evangelista is excellent at this strategy. She recommends to the buyer that they come in with a strong initial offer and she then tells the other side, "My client has been educated about the market and sees the value in the home which is why he is offering very close to list price. However, you should know that this is close to the top of what he will pay." Most sellers appreciate this candid approach and Yolanda's transaction immediately starts on a smoother playing field. Her goal is always, win/win.

Now, of course, in a buyer's market, a buyer could take advantage of the situation, low-ball and "steal the house." In my experience however, the buyer will pay for it in the long run. In this situation, what normally happens is that a seller who feels they have been robbed will often say, "Ok then, but I'm selling the house 'as is.' Don't even think about coming back to me with inspection issues because I'm not spending another dime." So it goes, with each side trying to gain ground on the playing field and with both losing in the end.

Let's look at the seller's side of this "wiggle room" now. Many sellers we work with unequivo-cally believe that they must overprice their home so they have room to come down. This is a terrible strategy however. Statistically, you will get the most money for your home when you price it close to what the market is indicating. In fact, even in a buyer's market, a well-priced home will often get multiple bids soon after being placed on the market.

As I counsel sellers, I believe the best strategy is twofold. First is to price their home to market, and second, is to then hold to that price. If it is priced correctly, I can defend that price and tell the other side, "As you can see, my clients have priced their home very competitively, but you need to know they are not going to be coming down a lot."

In the United States, real estate transactions are one of the last bastions of "haggling." Our team sometimes works with buyers and sellers who won't feel good about a transaction, unless they've "beaten" the other side. But the truth is that after guiding hundreds of transactions over the years, we can tell you that the best "deals" were ones that were win/win.

CHAPTER 14

Navigating Contracts, Disclosures, and Agency

Ignorance is *Not* Bliss—It's the Stuff of Lawsuits

Contracts signed without an understanding of the implications, or an undisclosed problem with your home can cause untold problems for you, at best holding up your closing and at worst, putting you in some very serious legal hot water. And the statement, "I didn't know" doesn't cut it in the vast majority of states. It is also vital to your interest to understand the laws of agency, or put another way, who represents (or doesn't represent) whom.

Contracts

Any discussion of contracts must be general in nature since what is customary and/or required will vary from state to state. If you are working with an agent, no matter the method of compensation, you will need to sign a listing contract which spells out the required duties of each of the parties and the amount and type of compensation due to the broker and how it will be paid. Make sure that you understand what you are reading and signing—if your agent has to explain it three times, so be it.

In addition, whether you are represented by an agent or selling on your own, there will be a variety of disclosure forms that must be completed and signed which I'll discuss in the next section.

Once you receive an offer, the customary contracts to be negotiated, completed, and signed will differ from state to state. In my home state of Massachusetts, we have a "two-step" process which consists of an *Offer to Purchase* with attendant contingencies and then, ten days to two weeks later, a final *Purchase & Sale*. Most states have a one step process. In Massachusetts, while the agent generally handles the offer, a real estate attorney will prepare and negotiate the final Purchase & Sale and an attorney will always be responsible for closing the transaction. Most states, on the other hand, use title companies. Again, make sure that you fully understand the procedures in your state.

Disclosures

Many homeowners are not aware that in most states, you, as a homeowner, are required to understand what needs to be disclosed regarding your home. Failure to disclose is serious business!

It's one of the reasons that I caution homeowners to think twice about taking on the job of selling their home alone, or buying into a limited service arrangement that has a harried licensee typing in your house information for a fee. I can guarantee you that for the short money they are being paid, as well as the fact that they owe you no fiduciary representation, this task will not include a careful review of what information is being typed in and what is or isn't being disclosed. Without representation, the homeowner is fully liable.

Think I'm exaggerating about the dangers that a lack of disclosure can bring? Then take a look at a couple of examples. One that was limited in its damages (since I, the listing agent, was responsible and paid for it), and one that resulted in very bad news for the unrepresented seller in question.

A few years back, I listed a home for a dear friend. I am generally very meticulous as to what I put into the MLS, but one detail that I forgot to disclose was that the home's water heater was rented. A buyer came along and put in an offer. At the subsequent home inspection; the rental status of this water heater came to light. The buyer made their offer for the house believing that the water heater was owned. So, guess who was buying a new water heater for these buyers? Yup, yours truly. Mistakes can be made even with a full-service, experienced agent. Can you imagine how many more mistakes are made with "limited service" agents who are not being paid enough to be thorough, or worse, a homeowner who's selling on their own?

I talked earlier about hiring referred professionals because they have accountability. In the above example, I made a mistake, but because I have a professional reputation that I am proud of and want to protect, I made the situation right. *There is a value in accountability.*

Now, let's take a look at a more serious example of a lack of disclosure. About five years ago, I brought some buyer-clients to a home that was being sold "By Owner" for a listed price of $425,000. My clients liked the home very much, and given that it was the height of a seller's market with a tremendous shortage of inventory, they decided to put in an offer immediately. I wrote up an offer (at full price mind you) and after a difficult negotiation with the seller (he not only wanted full price but he also wanted the buyers to pay my fee out of their pocket), he finally accepted my buyer's offer.

At the home inspection a few days later, the inspector pointed out several places where the ceiling had what appeared to be, water stains. Sure enough, when he went up to the attic, his moisture indicator showed that many of the boards were damp. Worse, he found evidence of water staining that came from an earlier time. I was surprised that this issue wasn't disclosed because roof leaks are a very easy condition for an inspector to discover. I was amazed that an owner, even one selling without representation, would not attend to, or at the very least, disclose a problem that he most assuredly had knowledge of.

I got together with the seller later that day so that I could discuss what was found. The seller claimed to have no knowledge of any roof leaks. I found that hard to believe, but I took him at his word. What really blew me away was that he refused to fix the leaks. The seller said, "Look, if they want the house, they will have to fix the roof themselves. If they don't want to, that's fine—I have a line of buyers behind them."

I replied, "You do understand that you are required now to disclose this issue to every subsequent buyer for your property." He smirked and said, "Yea, right. Like in this market I'm going to have any trouble finding another buyer." I could tell that he wasn't taking what I was saying very seriously. And my buyers weren't about to have to pay for repairs on the roof when they were already paying full price for the house. The seller returned their deposit and I found my buyers another home.

This is a perfect example of the problems that sellers run into when they try to negotiate and navigate the process on their own. We agents do real estate for a living, we know what to look for and what questions to ask. The seller figured that since he had a property to sell in a hot market, he could avoid repairing his roof or even disclosing that a problem existed.

Had the next buyer that came along been unrepresented and naïve enough to buy the home without a good home inspection, perhaps he could have gotten away with getting his property sold without disclosing the roof leak, although he would have some serious legal liability once the property closed and the first heavy rains came. After all, it wouldn't take much investigation to find out about the existence of my buyers—the seller had bragged to all his neighbors about how he sold his house to my buyers the first day.

As it happened, the next interested party that came in were buyers who were also represented. The first question their buyer agent asked is, "How come your house is back on the market?"

The seller was forced to say, "Oh, there's a minor leak in the roof and the buyers got all freaked out—but the leak is very minor." Now the red flag was up—the buyers and their agent began to wonder what *else* this seller had not disclosed. They walked away without even putting in an offer.

Had the seller done the repairs (since he considered them minor) at the beginning, or at the very least, disclosed a condition that after my buyers inspection report, he now had irrefutable knowledge of, he probably would have sold his property to these subsequent buyers. But, because of his ignorance of the law and real estate practice, and worse, arrogance when explained the facts, his property languished on the market for three months. He finally hired an agent who told him on no uncertain terms that he better fix the roof or disclose the problem if he wanted her to market his listing. He ended up fixing the roof *and* selling his property for $375,000—a $50,000 loss that could have been avoided by a $500 repair, or even, a disclosure of the condition which would have cost him nothing!

Most real estate professionals will nip the issue in the bud by having the seller fill out a Seller's Disclosure of Property Condition which covers all major mechanical and structural issues in the home and asks if the seller knows of an issue with each. In fact, a Seller's Disclosure is required in many states.

Should You Do a Pre-Inspection?

As the market slows down, I have been recommending of late that our sellers consider having an inspection done on their property prior to it going on the market. There are pluses and minuses of doing a Pre-Inspection. Clearly, whatever is discovered will have to be attended to or disclosed. Most buyers will have their own inspection anyway, but the benefit is that any items discovered can be addressed without pressure. In a slower market, I believe that a Pre-Inspection report, sitting on the table with the feature sheets, gives a prospective buyer a good feeling about the house and the sellers, and hopefully, it gives the property a competitive edge.

Environmental Disclosures

As a homeowner, you are expected to have knowledge of sewer regulations, the Lead Paint Law, radon, mold, and carbon monoxide. Yes, the list just keeps growing and unless real estate is your full time job, it is difficult to keep up to date on laws and disclosure.

If you do not have a listing agent who is representing you, consider hiring a real estate consultant who, for an hourly fee, can review with you the necessary forms and disclosures required by your state. If you cannot find a consultant in your area, even though it will generally cost more, make sure you confer with a real estate attorney.

Agency

I've saved this "big enchilada" for last. Agency is a topic that I am passionate about because I have seen too many buyers (and more and more of late, sellers) get taken to the cleaners financially because they made erroneous assumptions that the agent they were working with was representing them. In fact, the agent was representing the other side, or was representing no one.

If you haven't bought or sold a home in the last few years, you may not be up to date on what has been happening in real estate as regards the changes in agency law. Agency or representation is one of the most misunderstood topics in real estate, not only by buyers but also by sellers.

It has always been important for buyers to understand agency because prior to the practice of buyer representation, almost every agent a buyer would work with was in fact, working for the seller. Point in fact, as was outlined in the book I co-authored with Ken Deshaies *How To Make Your Realtor Get You the Best Deal*, various states began requiring agency disclosures because buyers were often not aware that "their agent" was, in fact, working for the seller.

I have always been a stickler about each party having their own representation because I cannot even begin to estimate the number of consumers I've met with over the years that have been royally screwed because they did not. In fact, when I'm the listing agent on a property and a buyer calls me directly to see it, I always ask them if they have an agent, and if they say no, I encourage them to get one. If they insist on seeing the home with me, I tell them, "I will show you the house but understand that I am representing the seller, so please do not say anything to me that you would not say directly to the seller themselves."

When I meet the buyer at the house, I will (as required by Massachusetts law) present them with a Consumer-Licensee Disclosure stating in writing that I am working for the seller and before asking them to sign it, I will "read" them, what I jokingly refer to as their Miranda Rights in Real Estate, "You have the right to your own representation. Without representation, anything you say can and will be used against you. If you don't have representation and want it, I can refer you to someone…"

Perhaps I go a little overboard on this. Most agents think I'm nuts to go to this degree, especially since I could "double-end" the deal by having the buyers buy directly with me, but I believe very strongly that consumers are best served when each side has an agent representing their interests.

With or without my encouragement, buyer agency is not going away. The most educated and qualified buyers (the ones you want) increasingly are asking for their own representation and all indications are that this trend will continue.

As a seller, do trust me on one thing—*buyers with their own representation should be welcomed not feared!* My experience has shown that buyers who have their own representation provide a much easier party to do business with than those who don't. Contrary to popular opinion, a buyer with their own agent is less, not more, likely to pick apart your home or make unreasonable demands. The reason is simple: a represented buyer has usually been educated about the buying process by their agent and they also are more likely to have been schooled on fair market value. As a listing agent, my experience is that when a buyer for my seller's property gives low-ball offers, makes excessive demands, and picks the house apart during inspection, they are usually not being represented and are taking their own counsel. Without an agent working in their interest, these buyers often overreach because they are "on their own."

For sellers today the widespread practice of buyer agency has changed the rules of the game. Today *sellers* need to be as cautious about what they discuss with agents who are not under contract to represent them as buyers should be. Unfortunately, most agents are not telling sellers that the rules have changed.

Let's take a look at the time-honored practice of prospective sellers asking several agents in for a listing appointment and discussing with each the price they need and want for their home. It's not that I have a problem with sellers interviewing agents—it is prudent for both sellers and buyers to take the time to interview agents before hiring one. But it is the discussion of a seller's wants, needs, and motivations with agents that are not under contract to represent them that poses a problem.

Before the widespread practice of buyer agency, a seller could have several agents in and hire only one, knowing that the others would still be "working for them" and could not use whatever was discussed against them. This is not the case anymore. Today, the seller chooses one agent and the agents that are *not* chosen can subsequently enter into a buyer agency contract with prospective buyers for that home. If it so happens that a buyer-client of one of those agents is interested in that particular home, that agent is free to share with their buyers anything that was said to them by the seller during the listing appointment!

This is why, over the last year or so, my team has stopped the practice of preparing a market analysis up front with a seller who is unknown to us. Now, when I am called by a seller to come "look at their house," I tell them upfront, "Mr. and Mrs. Seller, my partner and I would be pleased to come over and discuss with you how we market homes and the general housing market. However, please be aware that in your interest, we will not be discussing your specific wants and needs regarding the pricing of your home or your motivations for selling unless and until we are under contract to represent you."

Most sellers are taken aback by this statement because they have almost never heard this from any other agent. I explain why, kind of reading them *their* "Miranda Rights." "Please understand that anything you say to an agent who is not under contract with you can be shared with a buyer that they may later represent who might be interested in your home. I would advise you to not talk about your wants, needs, or the specific pricing of your home with any agent, until they are under contract to represent you."

CHAPTER 15

Negotiating the Deal:

The Best Real Estate Transactions are Win/Win

There are tons of books already written about successful negotiating so this will be a short chapter, but don't let brevity fool you into thinking that negotiating a real estate offer is either unimportant or something that can be done successfully by anyone. On the contrary, as I've said earlier, if you are going to hire a real estate professional for just two things—negotiating is one of them (troubleshooting the transaction is the other one and the subject of the next chapter).

The successful negotiation of offers is a skill that is definitely honed with practice. It involves knowledge of the process, dates, and terms as well as price. It requires a solid understanding of what is and what is not reasonable regarding the timing involved for an inspection, the language and dates regarding the buyer's loan commitment, and what contingencies are not in the seller's best interest. As we agents often say, "It's not the dollars but the terms that can kill you."

Successful negotiations also involve an ability to stay objective on your largest financial asset—a home that you may have put years of love into. This has nothing to do with talent or skill. I've seen many hard-nosed attorneys totally lose their cool when trying to entertain and negotiate offers on their own homes. For the record, I consider myself an expert negotiator for my clients, yet when it came time to sell my own home, I turned into the classic outraged seller, "What do you mean they only offered $_____. Don't they appreciate my home? Tell them to go take a walk!"

There's an old saying that any attorney who'd represent themselves has a fool for a client. It's no different in real estate and why most agents have a colleague negotiate offers on their own homes. Negotiation of offers is *absolutely where sellers, going it alone, often either give the store away or blow a deal that could have been successfully negotiated by letting their emotions take over.*

If you are either going it alone or, as can sometimes happen, you have found a buyer on your own without putting your house "on the market," don't let an inflexible commission system keep you from getting the help you need in the critical area of negotiating. Many real estate consultants can provide expert negotiating for an hourly fee capped at whatever number of hours you're comfortable with. This is a great option when you don't want or need any marketing assistance. *Wow, I've found my own buyer—now, what do I do?*

Assessing Your Priorities

Hopefully, I have convinced you of the wisdom of hiring a professional to negotiate any offers on your home, but that doesn't mean that you don't have some homework to do. Assessing your priorities should be done before you ever put your house on the market. It's best to think through what's important to you when you are not in the heat of the moment.

In assessing your priorities, ask yourself these questions:

- What terms of this sale are most important to me?
- Is it the ultimate sales price or how quickly my property sells?

- What is the small stuff that I wouldn't sweat?
- What is a deal breaker for me?

Often times, sellers can "trade" something that is not important to them (like appliances) for something that is (a higher price).

My "Have-No-Regrets" Exercise

Regarding a sales price, you might find it helpful (again, before you ever get an offer) to do the following exercise. Come up with a dollar figure that is the lowest sale price that you believe you could/would accept. Then test that price by thinking through a scenario where a buyer makes an offer on your property and you counter with this final figure and say, "Take it or leave it—this is the lowest I will go." Then think through two different outcomes:

1. The buyer accepts your final offer. Will you a) be happy because you sold your house at a price you can live with OR b) start thinking to yourself that you should have made that final "drop dead" price higher. Because if you are having second thoughts, that final price wasn't the right one.

2. The buyer rejects your counter-offer and moves on. Will you a) be disappointed but know that you couldn't have gone lower OR b) start thinking to yourself that you shouldn't have held out for such a high price. Because again, if the answer is b, that "drop dead" price wasn't right.

I have buyers do the same exercise, only in reverse: come up with a price that is the highest that they think they can pay for a house they are interested in. Test that dollar figure by thinking through what they might feel if the seller either accepted or rejected their offer.

I call this my "Have-No-Regrets" exercise because when it comes to real estate negotiations, the best deal is the one that you have no regrets about when all is said and done.

In the End, Make it a Win/Win

Unlike some fields, real estate negotiations are the best when each side feels they have given something but gotten something in return. My colleague and friend, Ken Deshaies said it best in his book, *Get the Best Deal When Selling Your Home*:

> The vast majority of real estate deals, when both sides are represented, should come down to what is fair. It should end up being a win/win situation, where everyone feels satisfied with the deal. We have all dealt with buyers who "want a deal" and who are unwilling to pay fair market value for any property. They want to steal it, to stick a knife in the seller's back and then twist it. They are only looking for someone who is vulnerable and has to sell at any price. We usually send away buyers like this.
>
> It is true some deals are made like this. We have found properties on the verge of foreclosure, or where sellers have to make a quick sale to save themselves from bankruptcy. We have not hesitated to get one of our buyers into such a deal. But your Realtor® is there to protect you from buyers who take the attitude that they can only be happy if you have "screwed" the seller. This attitude is really just corruptive of the whole process of real estate.

CHAPTER 16

Troubleshooting the Transaction

Nothing Else Matters if the Deal Doesn't Close

If you're like most consumers that I speak with, you might believe that the most difficult part of getting a home sold is putting it on the market and finding a buyer. But those of us who practice real estate for a living will tell you that the crucial period of time is *after* you have a signed offer. From "contract to close" is when a good listing agent plays the role of a quarterback, directing all the activities on the field and doing their utmost to execute a winning game plan resulting in a smooth and successful closing.

The reason most sellers focus on the period up to getting an offer is because that is when the visible work is being done. Preparing the home for market and the flurry of marketing activities and materials produced to get the word out gets all the attention. A quality agent's most important work is quietly done behind the scenes after the offer is accepted. It's kind of like an iceberg—the visible part above the water is actually a very small part—what lies below the surface (where the sharks are) is the work that will often make all the difference between whether you have a smooth transaction that closes on time, a myriad of problems, or a transaction that falls apart leaving you to start all over again.

From acceptance of the offer to close, the "devil is in the details." It's the attention to those details that separates the boys from the men and the girls from the women. Here's a look at a small sampling of items that need to be attended to and monitored:

- Are the buyers making application for their loan as specified in the offer, or are they still checking out lenders?

- Are the issues raised at inspection reasonable, or is the buyer trying to renegotiate the sale?

- If the buyer has a home to sell, is someone keeping tabs on that other home's status?

- Has the appraisal been ordered in a timely manner?

- If the appraisal comes in low, will there be someone with the knowledge of the market to be able to make a case to the buyer's lender?

- Are certain obligations that are required for closing— fixing issues raised at inspection, smoke detector and carbon monoxide certificates, and water and oil readings—being attended to?

- Is someone "riding herd" on the buyer's commitment to make sure that it is forthcoming by the date agreed?

These are just some examples of issues that, while seemingly small, can blow up a transaction late in the process and force a seller to start all over again, putting their house back on the market. What a disaster this can be if the seller has already scheduled a closing on their next home and they need the funds on this one in order to close!

Riding herd on these issues is not difficult but it does require time and attention to the details, which is not an easy task unless you are familiar with the process and selling a house is your only job. This is why I list *troubleshooting the transaction* as one of the four big potholes in selling a home and why a seller would be well advised to get help from a professional.

Having a quality listing agent is still no guarantee that problems won't arise. In the selling section on my team's website, I wrote the following:

Selling your home is like taking an airline flight cross country. When you start on your trip, you have no idea how the trip will go. Neither does the pilot! You could run into fifty different types of turbulence, or you could have a smooth flight and land on time. Certainly, the pilot will try to use his or her experience to navigate around storms and go for the smoothest flight plan, but if they're honest, they can't promise a turbulence-free trip. Their job is to get you to your destination in the least time and with the least aggravation while keeping you informed throughout the trip.

As your real estate consultants, we see ourselves as the pilot of your plane. Our job is to assist you in getting your home sold for the most money, in the least time, with the least aggravation. We can't promise you no turbulence, but we can promise that we will utilize our experience and expertise to take you on the smoothest flight that we can. *And if we do hit turbulence, we won't bail out on you.* We'll be your teammates throughout the flight until we get you safely to your destination.

Over the years I have spoken with many sellers who are trying to sell on their own who tell me that when the time comes, "their attorney will attend to that stuff." I have the highest respect for quality attorneys and I count several as good friends, but in the same way that I don't practice law, attorneys are generally not full time Realtors® *(if they're doing real estate full time, you have to wonder about the health of their law practice).* An attorney is not a good party to depend on to keep an eye out for all the real estate details that must be monitored—that is not what they do. Troubleshooting transactions *is* what Realtors® do. An experienced agent is very good at anticipating the inevitable potholes along the way and seeing that they're addressed so they don't blow up transactions.

You, as a seller, might have a relatively simple transaction, have everything go as planned, and close with success. You may not need any help as long as there are no issues. The problem is that most issues don't raise their ugly head until you're well along in the process. It's like the question, "Do you need fire insurance?" The answer is no, if you never have a fire. We, as smart consumers, buy insurance so we have the peace of mind to know that if we have a fire, we have the means to deal with it. It's the same with your transaction. Paying a good real estate professional to ride herd on the transaction is short money for the security of knowing that you'll be spared "surprises" late in the game. Along with negotiations, there are an increasing number of real estate consultants who can provide this assistance for a very reasonable fee.

E P I L O G U E

In 1995, as the designated "up agent"*, I received a call in my real estate office from a gentleman introducing himself as Harry Wilson. Mr. Wilson stated that he was looking to sell his home and needed an agent to come over and give him a price opinion. Being brand new in the business, I jumped at the opportunity and set an appointment to come over the following day.

As I drove up to his home at the appointed time, I was struck by the "curb appeal" of his rather modest ranch house and the beauty of the grounds. It was immediately clear to me that the splendor of the small yard didn't come from any professional landscaping, but rather from the obvious pride of owners who lovingly tended to their garden year in and year out.

---

*For years, traditional real estate offices have provided their agents with a built-in, but rather passive method for getting new leads. Called "floor time" or "up time," the practice has new or less-productive agents (who have the time) take turns answering the phones, and if any ad or sign calls come in, it is theirs. Of course, since 90 percent of the calls coming into offices are not ad or sign calls, rather calls for individual agents, the company gets plenty of free receptionist help. With the growth of buyer agency, this activity has become far less effective as a lead generator in recent years.

Mr. and Mrs. Wilson greeted me warmly at the door and invited me in. Mrs. Wilson said that she had just baked some cookies (she didn't have to say a thing—I could smell them!) and would I like to sit down and have one with a cup of coffee? I responded that that would be very nice and she immediately turned and went into the kitchen to put on some coffee. I suggested in the meantime that Mr. Wilson give me a tour of their home—given the small size of the house, I figured that the tour would take fifteen minutes tops and then we could all sit down and discuss their needs.

It became immediately apparent, as Mr. Wilson took me from room to room, that the tour of this small home would take a lot longer than fifteen minutes. As we entered each room, Mr. Wilson shared detailed memories of his family's thirty year history in this house. Each room had its own story. His son had broken a window in his room from a foul ball he hit when playing in the side yard. The counter in the home's only bathroom was permanently stained from some cosmetics his daughter had spilled on it so many years ago.

What struck me the most though, was the delight that Mr. Wilson took in describing the features of each room. The term "pride of ownership" would be wholly inadequate in characterizing this personalized tour—especially when he described how he had built the fireplace mantle and bookshelves in the family room himself, the enormous workshop in the garage, and the extensive built-in desk and shelf unit in the basement to accommodate his wife's sewing machine and craft materials. On top of all this, each room had curtains, hand-sewn by Mrs. Wilson, and wallpaper, long since gone out of style, hung by Mr. Wilson himself. I got the impression that every bit of decorating, improvement, or maintenance done to this home over 30 years was done by the Wilsons themselves.

When we got back to the kitchen, it was clear that Mr. Wilson's workmanship was most prominent here. What looked to be a small, rather ordinary kitchen instantly became transformed as Mrs. Wilson showed me one drawer that

Mr. Wilson had built to accommodate spices, and then showed me how many of the shelves had been crafted into "pull-outs" years before it was in vogue.

Before sitting down for coffee and cookies, Mrs. Wilson took me out to the back yard and showed me a large vegetable garden with ripe tomatoes and zucchini, and a separate section where freshly grown herbs scented the air. It was all, in a word, amazing.

When we finally settled in at their small table in their humble kitchen, Mr. Wilson commented how it would be impossible to ever replicate their home anywhere else. Mrs. Wilson added that whenever they had experienced bad times over the years, they had always been able to cut back here and there and cover their mortgage payment. She said, "We came of age in the Depression and our home has always been everything to us. When Harry's hours at the plant would periodically be cut back, we would make do with less, but we would always cover that mortgage payment every month. You see, we were the first in our families to actually own a home, and nothing was bigger to us than having a place we could call our own."

Out of respect for the newness of our relationship—after all, I was a virtual stranger—I had been hesitant to ask the obvious question burning in my mind, but I could no longer hold back: "Please forgive me, since we hardly know each other, but it seems very clear to me how much you both love your home. May I ask... why are you selling?"

Mr. Wilson looked down at his hands and said softly, "I was laid off from the plant a couple of months back. We've since been living off our savings, but this time, well, my job is not coming back. It's gone. After so many years, we just can't afford that mortgage payment and the taxes are killing us. I'll be damned if I'll ever see my house foreclosed on." It was obvious by the choke in his voice that this proud man was fighting back tears.

I was new in the business, but I couldn't stop myself and just blurted out, "I can't make any promises, but I work with a super lender. If she was able to restructure your mortgage, so that you could make the payments, would you stay put?" They both looked up at me, as Mr. Wilson replied, "In a New York minute."

This story of the Wilsons has a happy ending—my lender *was* able to restructure their loan so they could stay in their home. Mrs. Wilson continued to cultivate the garden she so loved while Mr. Wilson spent his days puttering in his workshop.

I will never forget how the Wilsons dropped by my office with a tin of homemade cookies soon after they got the news from my lender. In front of co-workers, Mr. Wilson asked how he could ever repay me—after all, I came to their home hopeful of getting a listing and walked away empty-handed. I had literally talked my way out of a job. I told Mr. Wilson that the best payment I could ever receive would be a referral to someone they know who might appreciate my services. As it happened, they turned out to be some of my best advocates until the end of their lives (Mr. Wilson passed away three years ago, and Mrs. Wilson followed a year later, may they be blessed).

I'm finishing this book with the story of the Wilsons because it illustrates the different ways that I get paid in my business:

1. I get paid by a commission or fee for a full transaction or by the hour.

2. I get paid by the transactions that come from referrals of my clients' friends, family, and co-workers who need my assistance (In fact, 100 percent of my personal business over the last three years has been exclusively by referral).

3. I get paid by a currency recognized by no financial institution—the feeling that comes from impacting people's lives for the good.

The real estate industry does not formally recognize that third method of payment. Given its sales focus, my industry has long been big on awards—for the greatest number of sales transactions (or transaction sides) completed in a year, a month, a week, the highest number of agents you can amass on your team, and most especially, the highest gross commission income collected in a year. (It has always fascinated me why the awards are on gross income rather than profit. It's a sad fact that many of the top agents winning multiple sales awards often have larger expenses than income coming in—hence, big sales numbers with the agents amassing debt along with the big awards).

I worked for RE/MAX for a few years and remember being puzzled about an award that was referred to as the "100 Percent Club." I finally asked my owner, "What does 100 percent mean?" He told me that the award referred to those agents that made at least $100,000 gross commission income in a year. I was appalled and wondered if I was the only one who felt uncomfortable. What other profession actually has an award that broadcasts to everyone how much money you make in a given year?

Over the years, I've never seen one award in my industry given for being a good dad, i.e., the agent who takes time off from his real estate practice to coach his son's little league team. I've never seen one award given to a mom who refers business to a colleague so she has time to be a leader for her daughter's Girl Scout troop.

Though we give lip service in real estate to providing good and attentive service, I've never seen an award given to an agent for choosing *not* to take on another listing or buyer because it would compromise the service they could give to their current clients. Unfortunately, the public has bought into this quantity-must-be-good mindset. I can't tell you the number of listings my team has "lost" over the years because a seller was convinced that the big-time agent that had For Sale signs all over town was the one to list with. Sellers often reason that since these agents are so busy, they must be the best. But the truth is that many of these "top" agents are experts at the numbers game that the industry encourages—taking on any buyer or seller that can fog a mirror, even if it means providing shoddy service because their time and resources are stretched too thin.

Can you imagine a physician being given an award at a medical convention for stuffing the greatest number of patients into their practice?

The reality is that hard-working agents are put into an untenable position daily—needing closed transactions to put food on the table, yet striving to step back, be objective, and put the client's needs first. Sometimes the goals converge—a seller needs to sell, a buyer needs to buy, and the agent is paid for the service they provide. And when this situation occurs it is a beautiful thing to behold. The seller gets the price they require, the buyer fondly imagines this house becoming their home, and the agent(s) have performed ethically, professionally, and earned their pay for a job well done. As agents, our job now is to know that doing the right thing is paramount, the referrals and rewards will follow, and homebuyers and home sellers will be given choices.

For more information on how
real estate agents can become consultants,
or to find a real estate consultant in your area,
please visit our website at
www.ACREcourse.com